MW01505202

THE BOSTON WAY

THE
BOSTON
WAY

*Radicals Against Slavery
and the Civil War*

Mark Kurlansky

GODINE

Boston

Published in 2025 by
GODINE
Boston, Massachusetts
www.godine.com

Copyright 2025 © by Mark Kurlansky

ALL RIGHTS RESERVED.
No part of this book may be used or reproduced in any manner
whatsoever without written permission from the publisher, except in
the case of brief quotations embodied in critical articles and reviews.
For more information, please visit our website.

LIBRARY OF CONGRESS CATALOGING-IN-PUBLICATION DATA

Names: Kurlansky, Mark author
Title: The Boston way : how radicals opposed slavery and the Civil War /
Mark Kurlansky.
Description: Boston : Godine, 2025. | Summary: "Nonfiction. History.
Abolitionism. Social Justice"-- Provided by publisher.
Identifiers: LCCN 2024033409 (print) | LCCN 2024033410 (ebook) | ISBN
9781567927658 hardback | ISBN 9781567927665 epub
Subjects: LCSH: Antislavery movements--Massachusetts--Boston--History--19th
century | Nonviolence--Massachusetts--Boston--History--19th century |
United States--History--Civil War, 1861-1865--Moral and ethical aspects
| Boston (Mass.)--History--19th century
Classification: LCC E450 .K87 2025 (print) | LCC E450 (ebook) | DDC
973.7/114--dc23/eng/20250328
LC record available at https://lccn.loc.gov/2024033409
LC ebook record available at https://lccn.loc.gov/2024033410

FIRST PRINTING, 2025
Printed in the United States

To everyone who has said no

*Big Elk and his companions soon discovered him
and came upon him with their war clubs. He stood
unarmed and quietly told them he had consecrated
himself by a vow to the Great Spirit, and could fight
no more. He gazed steadily in the face of his enemy,
and said if they wanted his life, they were welcome to
take it. The deep, mournful supernatural expression
of his eyes inspired them with awe. They thought
him insane.*

—Lydia Maria Child, "She Waits in
the Spirit Land," 1847

CONTENTS

James Wallace Black photograph of John Brown in Boston, 1859.

1859—
POTTAWATOMIE
IS BACK

They are slaves who fear to speak
For the fallen and the weak;
They are slaves who will not choose
Hatred, scoffing, and abuse,
Rather than in silence shrink
From the truth they needs must think;
They are slaves who dare not be
In the right with two or three.

—James Russell Lowell, 1843

In 1859, a critical year, word came that Old Pottawatomie was coming to Boston—again. This wasn't welcome news to the old Boston Clique, who were struggling to uphold their creed of nonviolent abolitionism. He'd arrived there two years before, upsetting some and stirring others. Only the year before, John Brown had become Pottawatomie Brown, the moniker from the Kansas creek where he and his sons hacked five men to death with swords and knives in front of their families. Not many wanted him back in Boston.

On his 1857 visit to Boston, Brown met with William Lloyd Garrison, the leader of the Boston Clique, the inner circle of Boston abolitionism, and publisher of the most important abolitionist paper in America. It was to be a meeting of two famous abolitionists, arranged by transcendentalists, the Clique's mostly like-minded colleagues in Concord.

The meeting was a disaster—a shouting match, according to some accounts. Brown thundered passages from the Old Testament about violence, vengeance, and the wrath of God. "What a convenient book the Old Testament is, when ever there is any fighting to be done," the leading abolitionist writer, Maria Child, once quipped. But Garrison fired back at Brown the teachings of Christ from the New Testament, about responding to evil with good and never with violence. It was not just a religious disagreement; it was a clash between two opposing concepts of political activism.

A slight-built, balding man with spectacles, Garrison did not have the dramatic look of Brown. Yet his cold, piercing blue eyes were a match for the wild man from Kansas. Like Brown, Garrison was a man of unwavering convictions.

When he returned in 1859, Brown did not look the same as he had two years earlier. Major portrait photographers had not been interested in this seemingly cracked radical in 1857. Some pictures of him had been taken in Kansas and other places, though—and all these photos showed his intensity. In one daguerreotype of Brown, from 1856 or '57, he looked particularly furious—his hair close cropped and clean shaven with nothing to soften his square jaw; thin, stiff, grimacing lips; and piercing stare—and that shot was later used as evidence that he was a madman.

When important people, such as Walt Whitman, came to Boston, James Wallace Black did a portrait. Black was one of the pioneers of photography. When Brown came to Boston in 1859, Black shot his portrait. There was a sense around the city that this Captain Brown was significant. He had taken the military title to gain respect, though he belonged to no military organization except his own.

The photo, which hangs in the National Portrait Gallery in Washington, DC, shows a fierce and angry man with a long beard and a thick mop of hair, in a defiant stance, his hands plunged in his pockets. He looked like a hawk, wings only slightly folded, about to pounce.

In this photo, his new great white beard evokes the Old Testament he was fond of quoting. Was he deliberately assuming the look of a biblical figure? Or was it just a disguise? A target of law enforcement, he had good reason not to want to be sighted by authorities in Boston. He often hid behind pseudonyms, sometimes calling himself Shubel Morgan (Shubel is a biblical name meaning a returning captive of God).

But why would a hunted man pose for a picture by a famous photographer? Photographic portraits were a new technology for this generation. For abolitionists, it sparked questions about celebrity. Should the personality or the idea be the star? One of their primary tools was speaking tours, and certain speakers became stars on the speaker circuit. Crowds would pack in to hear them.

Maria Child avoided having her picture taken. She was entirely engaged in presenting her ideas as a writer and had no interest in public speaking. On the other hand, Frederick Douglass, the most famous escaped slave and leading Black spokesman, saw the propaganda value of photographs. He was probably the most photographed American of the nineteenth century. Photographs displayed his powerful, regal looks, and his facial expression always denoted great seriousness. For Douglass, photography was a tool against the racist stereotype of the jolly negro. But like Brown and unlike Child, he also had an enormous ego and liked the idea of spreading his image. There is a correlation between charisma and egotism. Brown, Garrison, and Douglass all had large egos. Ralph Waldo Emerson, of no small ego himself, once wrote in his diary that men like Garrison, if they lost their egotism, "would lose their vigour."

Perhaps Brown posed for posterity. He was out to make history, and he wanted his face to be known. He believed in predestination and was certain that he was about to achieve his destiny. That destiny worried the Boston abolitionists, though they did not know exactly what it was. Brown was secretive.

Brown started out much like his peers—a New England-born abolitionist. He was not only determined to end slavery but also to champion the rights of Black people, women, and Native Americans. But very much unlike Brown, the Boston abolitionists were adamantly opposed to any use of violence. They had built a nonviolent movement.

They were a tight group of friends—men and women, Black and white—who had dinners and teas together; wrote letters to each other; and organized boycotts, protests, and speeches, huge rallies in Faneuil Hall, and extensive campaigns on the road in slave-free states. Their central belief, though some wavered and an increasing number had begun to disagree, was that emancipation must be accomplished without violence. Beyond a deep-seated moral conviction that nonviolence, the way of Christ, was the only true Christian path, there was a more pragmatic belief that only by nonviolently persuading slaveholders to change their ways would Black people be able to attain their rights. The Boston Clique believed that if slaves were freed through violence, it might take one hundred years for Blacks to gain their rights. Violence does not persuade. It hardens positions. A civil war was the colossal tragedy they were trying to avoid. But to Brown, violent conflict was the path to victory.

Nonviolence always has stiff opposition. Over the thirty years Garrison spent developing this movement, he constantly struggled to convince those opposed to slavery to oppose violence too, even though their adversaries wouldn't hesitate to take up arms. But as men like Brown lashed out with violence, other abolitionists felt the need to defend them, and it became more difficult to maintain the principle of nonviolence.

There had always been fissures. Samuel Gridley Howe, a doctor and a respected abolitionist, had famously fought in the Greek revolution. Maria Child's husband, David, who was at the heart of the Boston Clique, had proudly fought for Spain. Such youthful military adventures were rarely denounced. They gave an air of romanticism, showed a dedication to progressive causes, and demonstrated that these men were truly committed to freedom. They also represented the soft underbelly of the nonviolent movement. In fact, Howe eventually became one of Brown's biggest supporters.

The bearded crusader was a direct threat to Garrison. With all the blows to nonviolence the abolitionists had struggled against, this John Brown, if he could get a real following, would be the final coup de grace to their pacifism. He was already making inroads.

Originally, to be an abolitionist, especially in New England, meant being nonviolent, or, as they liked to say, "nonresistant." John Brown followed that path at first. He was an early organizer of the Ohio Underground Railroad, aiding the escape of refugee slaves. But he'd grown frustrated, concluding that nonresistants just talked a great deal. What was needed was action, he decided, and the more violent, the more frightening, the better.

Brown was often dismissed as a crackpot, but when he visited in 1859, the Boston abolitionists saw disturbing signs that some people, even their friends, the transcendentalists, were beginning to take him seriously. In February 1857, Ralph Waldo Emerson, a leading transcendentalist who generally opposed violence and even disliked the military, called him Captain Brown, a title only Brown had conferred on himself, and wrote that the captain had given "a good account of himself in Town Hall last night, to a meeting of citizens."

Garrison's clique was a small group, few enough to fit in a living room for tea. Other Bostonians and abolitionists from other parts of New England and even other parts of the country as well as British abolitionists often dropped by at these teas to discuss the nonviolent tactics of the cause. Members came and went.

Garrison and his paper were popular with Black people, and there were a number of them, aside from Douglass, in the Boston inner circle. There was William Nell, who integrated Boston public schools and joined Douglass and Garrison on freedom rides to integrate Boston commuter rails; Charles Lenox Remond, a celebrated abolitionist speaker; and Susan Paul, a Boston school teacher turned fiery activist. These were among the first Black people ever to address white audiences. They were nonviolent.

The Boston Clique spread their beliefs throughout the country through political activism, speaking tours, and writing. They planned their strategies over tea in Boston. Beautiful, fair-haired Bostonian Maria Chapman and her husband hosted many of their teas. She was from a distinguished family and British-educated in an age when Boston women did not have access to education. She was a respected writer on the subject of nonviolent abolitionism.

Garrison's paper, *The Liberator*, was the principal forum for abolitionism. Even Brown followed it and used to read it to his children. Douglass, despite a violent slave upbringing, believed in nonviolence and spread his ideas through eloquent speaking and powerful autobiographies read by thousands. Self-educated Maria Child, the most widely read of them, a leading American writer, was the embodiment of the concept they called "moral suasion," convincing slave owners of their error.

In Concord, the transcendentalists were centered around Ralph Waldo Emerson in his large white house with his philosophy of individualism. The group included Henry David Thoreau; celebrated feminist Margaret Fuller; Bronson Alcott, father of the later more famous Louisa May Alcott; and Elizabeth Peabody, the first woman publisher in America. The transcendentalists were abolitionists and believed in nonviolence; they even opposed war, but had a deep belief that an individual had to stand up for what they considered right. This belief opened a certain weakness toward Brown, whom they saw as a principled

man of action, though sometimes misguided or possibly men-
tally unbalanced.

Brown did not fit comfortably with either the abolitionists or
the transcendentalists. Many of the activists in both groups were
wealthy men who had their clothes tailored in London. Wendell
Phillips, a high-born Boston aristocrat, was an activist living in
a mansion in the most prestigious part of town. The fact that
they had money was what attracted Brown, since he was trying
to raise funds, but it did not make him feel close to them.

He wore the frayed, rough clothes of a failed farmer, which is
essentially what he was. He was poorly educated and wrote with
misspellings and bad grammar, although a number of notable
Boston writers of the day, including James Russell Lowell and
Emerson, credited his writing with distinct forcefulness. Henry
David Thoreau, Harvard educated like many of the transcendentalists and abolitionists, sneered while Brown was visiting
Boston, "He did not go to the college called Harvard, good old
Alma Mater as she is. He was not fed on the pap that is there
furnished." Even in 1857, the famously anti-war Thoreau was
beginning to sound like he was shifting over to Brown's violent
abolitionism. Pottawatomie Brown was creating a rift that had
not been there before between Boston abolitionists and Concord
transcendentalists. On this 1859 visit, there was a risk that the
divide would become even greater.

To Brown, they were a bunch of rich people who talked a lot,
and they were too fancy for his taste. Brown had not only failed as
a farmer; he had also failed as a shepherd, tanner, horse breeder,
lumber dealer, real estate speculator, and wool distributor. He
and his family were subsistence farmers living on a modest plot
of land in upstate New York. They produced nothing for sale and

struggled to meet their needs. His political action was sustained by fundraising trips such as the ones to Boston.

These Boston abolitionists were not all as wealthy as Brown thought. Brown might have identified with Maria Child, a baker's daughter who wore drab dresses and a dowdy bonnet. Her friends ridiculed her for her bonnet, and she said that once all the slaves were freed, she would get a new one, but she never did. William Lloyd Garrison came from a working-class background in nearby Newburyport, but he was a fastidious man who looked like a professor, and not at all like John Brown.

Though Brown could be soft-spoken, even kind to children, his ferocity was never well hidden. He was a sinewy man of average height. At the dinner table, he ate sparingly, rejecting most food, explaining that he had to keep lean for the great missions he would undertake. The Bostonians looked at this scruffy man with the long beard and blood on his hands with uncertainty. Author Herman Melville, a New Yorker married to the daughter of a famous Boston judge, called him "weird John Brown."

In 1857 Kansas broke into real warfare. And this drove a deep wedge in the abolitionist movement. Slaveholders from neighboring Missouri sent in armed bullies, known as "ruffians," to threaten the abolitionists. Northern abolitionists moved in to ensure it became a free state. In Boston, some abolitionists were sending blankets and food to the abolitionists in Kansas, but others were sending weapons.

Now, in 1859, the Kansas war was over. A new governor had driven out the Missouri ruffians and established Kansas as a free state. This was met with some relief in Boston. Kansas was not to be the beginning of a civil war.

Brown had some kind of plan but seemed intentionally vague on what it was. What did weird John Brown want in Boston now, in 1859, a year when peace could still be hoped for but seemed unlikely? It was hard not to believe that he was out to blow apart the Boston peace movement. Many still thought Brown was unbalanced, but he had shown in Boston a certain worrisome ability to convince a few people. Suppose he could convince enough people. What is a greater threat to a people with a dream than a man with a destiny.

Lydia Maria Francis, age twenty-four, in an engraving after the 1826 oil portrait by Francis Alexander.

One

1824—
LIFE IN ATHENS

Allow me to congratulate you on your arrival in Boston,
which, whether styled "the city of notions," "the Athens
of America," or, more pretentiously, "the hub of the
universe," is certainly second to no other on the score
of intelligence, patriotism, and love of freedom.
—William Lloyd Garrison to Edwin M.
Stanton, US Secretary of War, 1865

Even in the harsh years of the American Revolution, the idea was there. It grew during the hated War of 1812. In the 1820s, the idea that America could solve its problems without violence took hold among a strong and growing minority. It struggled on, challenged by tumultuous times. By 1859 the belief was in deep trouble; by 1861, when the shooting war began, there was little resistance; and by 1863 nonviolent abolitionism was completely smothered. Looking back, the 1820s seemed to be an age of innocence.

In 1824 the Reverend Convers Francis Jr. invited David Lee Child to one of the evenings in his home in Watertown, on the Charles River neighboring Cambridge. Convers was a Harvard-educated minister who relied on his alma mater connections to put together evenings with intellectuals of diverse and often unorthodox ideas. In the genteel setting of Convers Francis's house, ideas were put forth that became radical movements for which Boston would be famous.

Francis was in no sense a radical. He was a moderate, politically, what today might be called a centrist. But he had a strong sense that he belonged to a unique generation that had something important to say. These young Americans had grandparents and parents who knew the hardships of a fierce revolution. They strongly believed that the sacrifice of their ancestors should not be squandered and that it was up to their generation to build a new society that lived up to the ideals of liberty and equality.

David Child was an example of the kind of people of his generation that Francis liked to gather. Child was convinced that America was failing to live up to its ideals, and he was angry about it. Though raised by farmers in rural West Boylston, Child was a Harvard graduate who had served as a diplomat in the US Embassy in Lisbon and quit his job to fight for Spain against the restored French monarchy and against monarchy in general. The Spanish lost, and he returned home a disillusioned idealist. He spoke fluently not only the classic languages but also Portuguese, Spanish, and French. Now back in Boston, he was much the same as he would be for the rest of his life: full of ideas and convictions but with no money.

At thirty, he was a handsome young man with strong features who could speak well and knowledgeably on politics and articulately on the cause of liberty. He'd rubbed elbows with important people in government and had spent time in Europe. Just a farm boy from West Boylston, he had become a sophisticated figure in a still slightly provincial Boston.

Francis found other young men at Harvard who he thought might someday be important. He had discovered an unusual student, an uncombed and disheveled young freshman with a sharp, prominent nose and piercing gray eyes: David Henry Thoreau. He was also impressed by Ralph Waldo Emerson, who at that time was simply Waldo Emerson. He had entered Harvard at the age of fourteen and established himself as somewhat of a prankster. Now, finishing school quite young—still a teenager—he seemed a little lost. He was questioning the purpose of his education. He would, of course, become a minister, like his father and grandfather, but Waldo also liked bold ideas, and there was something slightly outrageous about him. These men in Francis's orbit were certain to shake things up.

They had been shaped by the American Revolution and the first fifty years of American history, which held the seeds of both abolition and antiwar sentiment. Some clung to the storied victories, especially in Massachusetts, such as Bunker Hill. But for many, the Revolution had been a violent eight-year conflict resembling a civil war. The country had been divided between "Loyalists" siding with Britain and "Patriots" seeking independence. Each side brutalized, publicly tortured, humiliated, and lynched the other. Both Loyalists and Patriots threw their opponents into dark and disease-ridden prison cells, from which many did not survive. Towns and communities and even families were divided. The death rate among American prisoners of war was the highest it has ever been in the country's history. The total wartime deaths of Revolutionary-Era Americans was five times higher as a percentage of the population than the losses a century and a half later in World War II. As always happens in the aftermath of a bloody conflict, the challenge was to show that the dead have not died in vain.

In Child's West Boylston during the Revolution, it was dangerous to let British sympathies be known. Loyalists in Massachusetts were stripped naked, and had hot tar poured over their bodies and feathers stuck to the tar. Often the feathers were set on fire. Those who survived this treatment took months to remove the tar, which stripped off skin with it, and were scarred for life.

Many of this new generation had family with harsh tales of the Revolution. The family of Francis's mother, Susannah, had been driven from their home in Charlestown by the Battle of Bunker Hill. Almost all their possessions had been lost in the fire from the battle. Convers Francis Sr. was from Medford, and his father, Benjamin, was one of the minutemen who had fought at Concord and Lexington. He was said to have killed five British soldiers, but he earned no money for fighting, and his wife and ten children were reduced to begging for food. Benjamin left the war before it ended and returned to Medford, where he resumed his trade as a weaver. His son, Convers Francis Sr., worked in a bakery, and in 1797, he seized an opportunity to buy out his employer. Convers Francis Sr.'s popular biscuits were the first crackers, or at least the first to be called crackers—Medford Crackers. The name comes from the fact that they were crisp and could easily be cracked into two pieces. Medford Crackers were extremely popular in New England, eaten with chowder. But the crackers were sold all over America and even in London.

Though his teenage years during the Revolution were difficult, Convers Sr. always honored his father as "a liberty man." He revered the ideals of the Revolution and believed passionately that if all men were created equal with inalienable rights, then slavery was a profound wrong and a violation of the principles for which so many had suffered, fought, and died.

There were others who felt this way in Medford as well. Before the Revolution, there had been Black slaves in Medford and Boston. At the time of the Revolution, 10 percent of Boston was Black. Slavery was not outlawed in Massachusetts until 1790. Massachusetts people, like Convers Francis Sr., who were born before or even during the Revolution, had a clear memory of slavery.

Medford became the first town in the new United States to protect a runaway slave. The man, Caesar, was a tailor, and he was originally rescued by the blacksmith Nathan Wait. This fit neatly into Convers Francis Sr.'s ideology: that it was the tradesmen—bakers, tailors, blacksmiths—who were the bedrock of the new country and would form the core of the abolitionist movement. Convers repeatedly told his children the story of Caesar and they were raised with an abolitionist message. Convers Jr. was open to the idea of abolition, though he was never really dedicated to the cause.

In 1812 America went to war with Britain once more. Historians are still arguing about exactly why. What we now call the War of 1812 was deeply unpopular in Massachusetts, where it was named "Madison's War" because President Madison had pushed for it. In 1814, James Monroe, the last Founding Father to become president, negotiated an end to the war and ushered in the first age of national unity. The somewhat ridiculous phrase "Era of Good Feelings" was coined by leading Boston journalist and Revolutionary War veteran Benjamin Russell, in his newspaper, *Columbian Centinel*, in 1817, when Monroe came to Boston as part of a triumphant national tour. The Era of Good Feelings meant that the darkness and pain of the years before were to be forgotten.

It was during this time that Americans like David Child, who wanted to talk about how America had gone wrong, were seen as marginal outcasts. The mistreatment of Native Americans was a major issue for some, but the majority of Americans did not want to let such topics upset the good feelings they were enjoying. Although Monroe, and even Jefferson before him, had discussed the possibility of negotiating the removal of Native Americans from southern lands to facilitate the expansion of European Americans, Andrew Jackson embraced this cause with an energy and ruthlessness not seen before. In 1814 he went to war against the Creeks, destroyed them, and forced them off their land. Between 1814 and 1824, Jackson, as a politician and as a military officer, negotiated nine treaties forcing tribes off of their eastern lands.

To dissidents such as Child, the abuse of Native Americans and the practice of slavery, both strongly backed by Jackson, were evidence of America's failure to live up to the Declaration of Independence. As Boston abolitionists started to organize, one of their first goals was to disturb the good feeling and raise consciousness about the abuse of Natives and the enslavement of Africans, which was not diminishing as Jefferson had predicted, but was increasing in the South along with the cotton industry.

At the time of Convers Francis Jr.'s invitation, David Lee Child was only recently back from his European adventure. He was pleased to join the gathering because it was an opportunity to renew Harvard connections in search of like-minded men who would work to reform America. He had been at the center of a European struggle between the old forces of monarchy and the new ones of liberty. For opponents of the reemerging monarchy, like Child, anti-monarchism involved the ongoing struggle to fulfill the ideals of the American and French Revolutions. Child was skilled at articulating this struggle and explaining Europe to Americans.

David Child had a lot to talk about at the dinner, but, if he were honest, the person he was most interested in meeting was Convers Francis's younger sister. Child was not the only one who wanted to meet Lydia Maria Francis in 1824. At the age of twenty-two, six years younger than Convers and eight years younger than David, she was a literary star. Her first novel, *Hobomok: A Tale of Early Times*, was a sensation that year. She was the first woman in America to author a historical novel, and she seemed destined to become one of the country's leading writers.

That same year, a meeting with the historian John Gorham Palfrey was the catalyst for her career. He was part of a movement that believed that in postrevolutionary America, a national literature needed to be created. Noah Webster was of the same mind when, in 1825, he completed a dictionary of the American language with distinctly American spelling and some words that only existed in America.

When Lydia Maria Francis met Palfrey one morning, he spoke about how a truly American literature would not be about Europeans but would focus on Native Americans and Puritans. She was so deeply moved by their conversation that by the time of afternoon prayers, she had already completed the first chapter of *Hobomok*. Her brother Convers read the chapter and asked, in an awed tone, "But Maria, did you really write this?" She finished it in six weeks.

Hobomok was a groundbreaking book. It is the story of the passionate affair between a white woman and a Native American, which was already controversial. This was not a James Fenimore Cooper "noble savage," too, but a very human Native American. And the woman, refusing to be "the fallen woman," leaves him, without remorse about the relationship. Lydia Maria was fearless. In fact, her fearlessness was her most striking characteristic. She even looked the part.

Unlike David Child, Lydia Maria Francis was not considered attractive by the conventional standards of the day. A New England beauty was supposed to be tall and blond, with eyes the bright blue of a cheerful day. Lydia Maria, of English stock with ancestors in America as far back as 1633, was short and dark with thick black hair and deep dark eyes that seemed to brighten when she angrily drove home a political point.

She was not like other women, nor did she want to be. Many men were infatuated with her. Celebrated Boston portrait artist Francis Alexander was drawn to her. At the time of the dinner party, she had been going to his studio for sittings, and he was painting her portrait free of charge. He preserved his fascination with her in oil on canvas. This painting is the most striking image we have of her today, her thick black curls worn around her head like a soft crown and her penetrating eyes staring off at a distant target.

Of five siblings, Lydia Maria, the youngest, was the only one to take her father's abolitionist position. Convers Jr., who was very close to Maria, gradually adopted this viewpoint, but without her passion. The oldest, James, was an overt racist and supported the proslavery position. The other two, another brother and a sister, were largely silent on the issue.

When Maria was twelve years old, her mother died. She wasn't close to her mother, who clearly favored Convers. Her life, dead at forty-eight after exhausting herself bearing seven children and caring for the five that survived, was more of a cautionary tale for Maria than that of a role model. It made her wary of marriage. But Maria felt deep guilt about having failed to comfort her mother when she was dying. They had fought only hours before she had died, and Maria walked out on her, a guilt that led to depression that Maria never entirely conquered. For the rest of her life, she was ready to nurse anyone who was ailing, as though to make up for the lapse with her mother.

Women, in the new revolutionary ideal, were taught to read and write, which was considered a radical step forward. But they were offered little education beyond that. Growing up, Maria lost herself in books. Her brother, Convers, was also a voracious reader. They read together and discussed ideas. He wanted to go to college. To his father, this was a wasteful, pointless pursuit, and it took a great deal of pressure from friends before he was allowed to go to Harvard.

Since women had no higher education available, Maria was educated by her brother Convers. She loved Shakespeare, the heroic tales of Sir Walter Scott and Milton. She thought *Paradise Lost* had "astonishing grandeur of description." But she also complained to her brother, "Don't you think Milton asserts the superiority of his sex in too lordly a manner?" Certainly, Milton's Adam and Eve are not equal partners. She had a keen ear for sexism and never remained silent on the subject.

When Convers left for Harvard, he arranged for Maria to move to their sister Mary's home on the northern Kennebec River in Maine in a village called Norridgewock, named after a nearly extinct group of the Wabanaki nation. Moving to Maine in the early nineteenth century sounds like a move to a remote backwoods. But even before the Revolution, when Massachusetts itself was a colony, Maine functioned as a colonial outpost of Massachusetts. Affluent Bostonians coveted inexpensive land in select areas of Maine, notably along the Kennebec. Even today, the area carries the place names of Boston aristocrats such as Hancock, Bowdoin, and Gardiner. Along with such aristocrats, Boston lawyers moved to the Kennebec to look after their interests while at the same time growing wealthy by buying and selling real estate. Maria's brother-in-law, Mary's husband, Warren Preston, was such an attorney. He had grown wealthy on Maine real estate and lived in a large, luxurious house. While Maria learned frontier skills, such as preserving food to get through the winter, making candles, weaving cloth, and child rearing, she also found herself in the company of college-educated people who debated the political and legal issues of the day.

Maria had been in Maine since 1815, but her last year there, 1820, was the critical one, politically. It was during this time that Maria witnessed her first abolitionist struggle. This was the year of the Missouri Compromise. Maine had applied for statehood, which would have meant more free states than slave states. The proslavery congressmen would only vote for Maine statehood if Missouri was granted statehood as a slave state, which violated the 1787 ordinance banning slavery in the new Northwest Territory. In Maine, an ardent abolitionist population was furious.

Abolitionists had accepted slavery in the Constitution with the belief that no new territories would allow it.

Many of the Founding Fathers, including slave owners such as Thomas Jefferson, believed that slavery would gradually disappear. But they had not foreseen the 1794 brainchild of Massachusetts-born inventor Eli Whitney—the cotton gin. Offering an efficient way to separate seeds from fibers, southern cotton became the leading American export, and New England textile mills were also leading customers. But there was no machine to grow and harvest cotton. That was done inexpensively with slave labor. They worked the land hard without rotating crops, squeezing out as much as they could, and this type of farming ate up fertile soil and created a constant need for new land to maintain a high level of production. And so slavers, rather than maintaining their land, looked for new land—more slave states. The Missouri Compromise, the fight Maria witnessed from Maine, was the first battle in a struggle that would consume America.

The rights of Black people were not her first concern in Maine. She was learning about the plight of Native Americans too. In the sixteenth and seventeenth centuries, when Europeans started coming to Maine, there were at least twenty thousand Indigenous people living in Maine, mostly of the Wabanaki tribes, and another sixty thousand Natives in the rest of New England. But brutal wars in the seventeenth and early eighteenth centuries, along with diseases, decimated the population throughout New England. When Maria moved to Maine, though, she started writing articles and stories about the Abenakis and the Penobscots, both tribes of the Wabanaki Confederacy, there were few left. This idea that she was living in Maine among the Wabanaki was largely a myth she created. Not far from Norridgewock, the remains of an Abenaki village lay near a riverbank. White farmers' ploughs would unearth broken pottery, hatchets, and other remnants. It was a favorite place for Maria to visit and contemplate and hear tales from the locals of the Abenaki. She also visited a small Penobscot village on the banks of the Kennebec. There she met their chief, who she called "Captain Neptune," and his family, who made a lasting impression on the curious teenager.

She saw a nobility in Neptune and was impressed by the physical strength of the women in his family and in the village. Maria believed that the frailty of women was a sexist myth and kept herself fit and healthy (she stayed active into her seventies).

In 1821 Maria accepted Convers's invitation to move in with him in Watertown. There, she began to change, starting with her name. She had never liked her given name, Lydia, perhaps because she disliked her namesake, her grandmother, who was married to "The Liberty man." Name-changing was fashionable at the time. The young writer Nathaniel Hawthorne had changed his name because his ancestor Hathorne had been a judge at the Salem witch trials, which were generally regarded as a disgrace. David Henry Thoreau switched around his first and middle names. Educator and transcendentalist Bronson Alcott had originally been Alcox, and Emerson changed his second wife Lydia's name to Lydian because he did not like the way Bostonians pronounced her name: Lydiar. Lydia Francis became Maria (pronounced Ma-RYE-a).

Conceding to the tradition of women writers for the past two centuries, she signed her first novel, *Hobomok*, "by an American." Some bolder women had signed their books "by a

Lady." Her second novel, *The Rebels*, was signed "by the author of *Hobomok*." But eventually she turned from these conventions and signed all her work "L. Maria Child," which was, by that point, a famous name.

Most people knew who wrote *Hobomok*. When the work was first published, the influential *North American Review* called it "revolting." Maria wrote to George Ticknor, a friend of her brother Convers and one of the *Review's* most influential contributors. "With trembling diffidence," she began her letter to him. Ticknor arranged for a second longer article praising the book, invited her to Boston to meet people, and soon the book was selling briskly.

It was always said that Ticknor would "make or break" new writers. Ticknor arranged for Maria to be invited to the leading homes in Boston. With her plain clothes and speech, the baker's daughter from Medford was a star in the kinds of homes she had never seen, with carpets from Asia and famous paintings hanging on the walls and women wearing sparkling baubles of family jewelry. Sophisticated Boston society was charmed by her lack of pretense and impressed with her wit and intelligence.

Dinners at her brother's house were probably far tamer than high society gatherings. Most Boston progressives, including Maria, disapproved of any kind of alcohol. They were evenings of quiet conversations, except for an occasional disagreement.

But even after frequenting evenings with the elite, Maria thought David Child was the most romantic man she had ever met. She thought he "possesses the rich fund of an intelligent traveller without the slightest tinge of a traveller's vanity." After another meeting, she wrote in her journal, "He is the most gallant man that has lived since the sixteenth century and needs nothing but helmet, shield, and chain armor to make him a complete knight of chivalry." And David thought she was the most fascinating woman he had ever met.

They dated regularly after that second meeting and talked. That first evening, they had talked about the rights of Native Americans, a subject on which she seemed to have some expertise, and the European situation on which he was an expert. Maria had never been out of New England and yearned to learn of other places. She was fascinated by a man who knew Europe and even spoke its languages. In subsequent meetings, conversations on Native American rights easily expanded to talking about the abolition of slavery. They also spoke about women's rights and politics, the tricks and side steps of government, and the loathsomeness of political figures like Andrew Jackson. But they also made each other laugh.

The dialogue continued for the next fifty years. In 1828 David and Maria got married. Maria's father, Convers Sr., was not pleased. David was a thirty-three-year-old without a secure income who borrowed money extravagantly. Worse, from the father's point of view, he was a lawyer who, instead of taking on profitable cases, of which there were many in Boston, spent his time defending impoverished clients who could not pay anything. Convers Sr. correctly prophesized that David offered a life of poverty. But it was also an exciting life, one of political engagement, of ceaselessly fighting the good fight, and of being at the forefront of Boston intellectual and political controversy.

William Lloyd Garrison, founder of The Liberator, *in the 1830s.*

Two

1831—
BEING HEARD

*Are we enough to make a revolution? No, but we are
enough to begin one.*

—William Lloyd Garrison

On the first day of 1831, from a grubby little downtown print shop, the first issue was launched of a cramped four-page publication that looked as unimpressive and unattractive as the shop where it was printed. It was called *The Liberator*, and for all its makeshift appearance, it marked the official launch of one of the great progressive movements of nineteenth-century America and contributed to Boston's growing reputation as a place where new ideas ripened.

In the 1820s Boston was the capital of the American printing trade. It was already becoming a vibrant center of nineteenth-century thinking. Philosophers, poets, novelists, journalists, theologians, and dissidents were published in Boston, and many of them lived there. New Englanders saw the city as the seat of the Revolution and therefore the home of the biggest ideas of the day. Bostonians tended to see it as the center of the universe. They used to say that the great dome of the statehouse perched on top of Beacon Hill was "the hub of the solar system."

All this was remarkable considering Boston was not one of the larger cities in the nation. It had a population of sixty thousand, which was only a third of the size of New York or Philadelphia. Children played on the mudflats that were later to become the neighborhood of Back Bay. The waterfront was teeming with rough-looking men who spoke in languages from around the world. Boston grew inward with great density in a limited space and narrow streets that did not lead directly to other places, forming a complicated web. The streets did not seem to have a plan. There were few main arteries. State Street went straight from the waterfront, passing near Faneuil Hall, to the Old State House and led the pedestrian or carriage travelers fairly efficiently to the Common, the principal park. But most streets were short and connected to other such streets at odd angles, creating a complex jumble of narrow passageways so that it took time to cover a short distance, making the city seem bigger than it really was.

It was a city of insular neighborhoods. One side of the Common was for aristocrats, and the other was a working-class district. One side of Beacon Hill was for affluent white people and the other side was for working class Black people and was called "Nigger Hill," a popular label that reveals a deeply embedded racist attitude of many Bostonians at the time. Boston grew because other neighborhoods such as Dorchester; wooded Brookline; and Cambridge, home of Harvard, whose students were mostly from Massachusetts, became unofficially part of Boston, while new bridges helped connect outlying places such as Medford and Concord. So there was a greater Boston far beyond the city limits.

Into this printing center in 1826 came William Lloyd Garrison, a twenty-one-year-old typesetter. Garrison came from Newburyport, a declining commercial port. Boston seemed huge to him. It was like a Dickensian scene of the young man arriving in London.

A stagecoach dropped him off by the waterfront, near Faneuil Hall, a neighborhood where, with only a few brief interludes, he would live and work for the rest of his life. It was the founding moment for the downtown group that would come to be called the Boston Clique.

At the age of thirteen, his family impoverished, his merchant sailor father having deserted them, Lloyd, as he was generally known, had begun work at his hometown newspaper, the *Newburyport Herald*. Such local newspapers were booming all over America, particularly in New England. There were more than fifty local newspapers in Massachusetts and more than 120 printing offices around the state.

Initially, the work was less than inspiring. Garrison boiled varnish and lampblack to make ink. Lampblack was soot from a lamp mixed with gum and water. The ink pots gave a pungent smell to the print shop and covered the ink maker with black smudges. But in time, he worked his way up to typesetter, a highly skilled job at which he became a master. He was following a typical path by which a working-class boy might eventually become a journalist, though not all typesetters rose to higher positions.

Metal type, each letter a single piece, was placed in a sloping box by the typesetter. With one hand, he'd choose type and with the other, place them in the composing stick, a metal strip designed to hold one line of printing. He had to place the type with spaces for the words—careful to avoid wide breaks, known as pigeon holes, but also not so narrow that the words ran together. It took great skill, and speed was important. It was said that Lloyd Garrison could set a thousand spaces in an hour with very few mistakes.

Although only a printer, Garrison was looking for ways to advance his strong political beliefs, especially abolitionism. He began his Boston career working as a printer for David Child, who was now editor of a progressive newspaper, the *Massachusetts Journal*.

But Garrison did not want to remain a printer. He had a burning passion to be heard on issues that stirred him. The son of a self-destructive alcoholic, he denounced alcohol and took a job in January 1828 as editor of a Boston temperance paper, the *National Philanthropist*. But after six months, he seized the opportunity to be editor of the *Journal of the Times*, an abolitionist paper in Bennington, Vermont. The paper folded in March 1829.

By this point, he saw himself as primarily an abolitionist. On July 4, 1829, he delivered his first public address on abolitionism at a Boston Fourth of July event. Abolitionists had a tradition of Fourth of July speeches.

That same year, a Quaker abolitionist, Benjamin Lundy, a harness maker who'd managed to start up his own paper, arrived in Boston on a national tour to discuss abolitionist efforts and to raise money for his paper. Lundy, who was based in Baltimore, described the work that was being done, including the organizing of antislavery societies. He had started his struggling little

Baltimore-based abolitionist paper, *Genius of Universal Emancipation*, in 1821. Lundy seemed an unimpressive man, small and soft-spoken, but Lloyd, who was now back in Boston, was drawn to what he had to say and the things he was trying to do. After meeting Lundy in Boston, Garrison decided to move to Baltimore and coedit Lundy's one-man paper. Garrison was impressed with Lundy's message, though not with his printing skills. In Baltimore, he witnessed the treatment of slaves firsthand and he boarded with free Blacks and heard their stories. Garrison's ideas on abolition solidified.

Lundy believed that slaves should be emancipated through a gradual process and Garrison became a passionate advocate of the complete and immediate emancipation of all slaves. It was a controversial position that was labeled "immediatism." Immediatists were the real radicals. The plan was for them to disagree and each sign his own editorials, and it worked cordially for about ten weeks.

The paper ceased publication because of a controversy inflamed by Garrison. He accused a Newburyport merchant, Francis Todd, of shipping slaves from Baltimore to New Orleans. This created a scandal back in Massachusetts, and the merchant sued for libel. Lloyd lost and, unable to pay the fine, was jailed. After forty-nine days, Arthur Tappan, a wealthy New Yorker who was to become a prominent abolitionist, albeit later on often in disagreement with the Garrison group in Boston, paid his fine.

In June 1829, at liberty, Lloyd Garrison had no paper and decided to start his own. He thought of publishing in Washington, the capital that was increasingly focused on debating slavery. But he decided that Boston was a better base because he believed he would have more success rallying Bostonians.

He would never again waiver from his decision to base his movement in Boston.

His plan was to start gathering support through a series of speeches. But it was difficult to find a venue for a speech by an unknown abolitionist pushing the controversial idea of immediatism. Eventually, he was able to arrange three speeches in Julien Hall, a new downtown space on the corner of Congress and Milk Streets in what is today the financial district. Julien Hall featured political events, art shows, and even animal shows.

Garrison argued for immediatism and attacked the American Colonization Society. This organization, founded in 1817, thought they were putting a kind face on abolition by arguing that slaves should be emancipated in small numbers at the discretion of slave owners and, once freed, should be sent off to start a new life in South America, the Caribbean, or West Africa. Anywhere but here. The argument against immediatism was that setting free large numbers of slaves, completely unsuited for the white American life, would create chaos.

Colonization had many distinguished supporters, including elderly Thomas Jefferson and James Madison and a young Abraham Lincoln. One of the founders of the Colonization Society was Henry Clay, a leading politician who claimed to be against slavery even though he owned slaves. The argument against colonization was that people born in the US had a right to live there. Colonization was deeply offensive to most free Blacks, and Garrison's strong stance on immediatism was one of the reasons he enjoyed robust support from free Blacks.

From these early speeches in 1829 and 1830 Garrison gained a loyal following. Samuel May, a Harvard-educated Unitarian minister from an elite Boston family, came to one of the speeches with his friends Samuel Edmund Sewall, a classmate of David Child at Harvard, and Bronson Alcott. Afterward, the four talked into the night, and Sewall and May became important lifelong supporters of Garrison. That speech was also attended by Ellis Gray Loring, a wealthy Boston lawyer who became a financial backer of Garrison's paper and who brought to the cause William Ellery Channing, the leading Unitarian in America.

This was how Boston abolitionism worked—supporters bringing in more supporters. Garrison's "radical" positions could easily have marginalized his group. There were other abolitionist groups around New England—in all the other New England states, as well as the Quakers. Opposing slavery was an obligatory Quaker belief. But because Garrison was able to bring in well-established and even affluent Bostonians, his abolitionist group became the one to listen to, whose members could not be ignored. The scrappy typesetter from Newburyport became an important Boston intellectual and a controversial political leader.

By the end of 1830, Garrison felt ready to start his paper. With one assistant, Isaac Knapp, a childhood friend and printer from Newburyport, he set up shop in Merchant Hall, a four-story brick building near the waterfront on the corner of Congress and Water Streets, only a short walk from where he first got off the stagecoach in 1826. On the ground floor was one of Boston's best food markets. From his ink-spattered window, he could see Faneuil Hall, famous for speeches by anti-British patriots during the Revolution and later both pro- and anti-abolition events. Looking farther, he could see the site of the battle of Bunker Hill across the water in Charlestown. Garrison would later say that he had launched his banner of liberty within sight of that battleground. It might seem odd for a pacifist to pay homage to a battle, but he frequently made such references because he understood that the Revolution had become sacred to most New Englanders, and he wanted to point out that he was fighting for the principles of the Revolution.

They printed the first paper late on New Year's Eve. They had to print at night because the type was borrowed and had to be returned in the morning. On January 1, 1831, Garrison and Knapp published the first issue of *The Liberator*, a crammed four-column paper on four pages. It was never beautiful, but the little publication made him famous and would be published every week until December 29, 1865.

Soon after they began printing, they found type of their own—a worn set in an old foundry—and a used hand press. They moved to a larger space in the building with two oak tables, two chairs, and two mattresses so that Garrison and Knapp could sleep there. Friends joked about what a dilapidated, ink-splattered hovel the shop was.

Garrison wrote most but not all of the articles. Sometimes he set the type as he was writing. Samuel Sewall said that "the liberator" sounded too aggressive and a better name would be "the Safety Lamp." But Garrison knew the tone he wanted. From the first printing, he made his stand:

> *I will be as harsh as truth, and as uncompromising as justice.*
> *On this subject I do not wish to think, or speak, or write, with*
> *moderation. . . . I am in earnest—I will not equivocate—*
> *I will not excuse—I will not retreat a single inch—AND*
> *I WILL BE HEARD.*

He demanded immediate freedom for all slaves and, unlike many abolitionists, full rights of citizenship. He also demanded the fair and equal treatment of Blacks in the North as well as the South. He called for the boycott of slave-made products and spoke out for the right to intermarriage.

A subscription to *The Liberator* cost two dollars a year. The paper was highly controversial for white readers but widely embraced by Blacks. Free Blacks had almost nothing to read that was not from the white point of view. Even abolitionist writing favored colonialism or other gradual formulas of emancipation. It was a widely held belief among white people, even young Abraham Lincoln, that Black Americans were not ready to fit in with white society.

A white society with such attitudes did not provide Black people with journalism they could trust. John Brown Russwurm, the first African American graduate of Bowdoin College and only the third African American to graduate from an American college, wanted to offer a paper for Black readers—the first Black-run paper. In 1827, four years earlier than *The Liberator*, with Samuel Eli Cornish, a free-born Black who grew up in Philadelphia, Russwurm began publishing, in New York, *Freedom's Journal*, a one-page, four-column weekly. It provided a Black view of events and had editorials on racism and abolitionism. Every week, it distributed more than eight hundred copies to eleven northern states.

But there were three hundred thousand free Blacks in the North and there was a hunger for more writing that reflected their point of view. Garrison's paper was his own point of view, and he intended it for Blacks and whites, hitting hard on an uncompromising immediatism, inviting editorials, attacking editorials in other publications—relentless. It happened to be what many Black readers wanted to hear.

The Liberator had only 500 subscribers its first year, of which 450 were African American. In time, the subscription list rose to 3,000, still mostly Black readers. Garrison proudly announced that it was a paper for people of color. "It is their organ," he said. The mayor of Boston, Harrison Gray Otis, a wealthy aristocrat of Revolutionary War pedigree, disparaged the newspaper by saying that it was only read by Black people.

But to Garrison, this was an accomplishment. To become popular in the Boston Black community with a message of nonviolent revolution, Garrison had to win over other arguments in the community. Some Blacks, even some of his readers, struggled with his unyielding opposition to violence. An opposing view had taken hold among many free Blacks, especially in Boston. In 1829, the son of an enslaved man and a free Black woman, David Walker, who had wandered through America and recently settled in Boston, created a sensation with his book, *An Appeal to the Colored Citizens of the World.*

Walker believed that Black people would only get their rights through violence. "The whites have always been an unjust, jealous, unmerciful, avaricious and blood-thirsty set of beings."

The white man does not know, according to Walker, "that there is an unconquerable disposition in the breasts of the Blacks." Walker wrote, "one good Black man can put to death six white men." He wrote that it was better to be killed than to be a slave. His message to white America was, "your DESTRUCTION is at hand, and will be speedily consummated, unless you REPENT."

Two years later, Lloyd Garrison was offering a different vision in *The Liberator* and it was becoming popular in the Boston

Black community. In only the second issue of *The Liberator*, Garrison took his stand on Walker. "Believing, as we do, . . . that a good end does not justify wicked means . . . , we deprecate the spirit and tendency of this *Appeal*." But he did not denounce Walker himself, saying that such calls for violence were caused by slaveholders and their supporters.

Garrison's influence went far beyond his subscription list. His articles were talked about, often denounced. *The Liberator* was banned in the South. The state of Georgia offered a $5,000 reward for his capture. Garrison constantly received death threats and even published some of them. In South Carolina, a $1,500 reward was offered for the capture of any white man caught distributing copies of *The Liberator*. But it wasn't necessary to distribute copies. Southern papers were full of news of the hated little paper from Boston. Some even reprinted his articles to show how heinous they were. David Child, in the *Massachusetts Journal*, referred to his former typesetter as "The lion of the day at the South" and described southern attempts to silence Garrison as "to turn the wind by blowing against it."

On the other hand, *The Liberator* would frequently carry writing by southern slavers, including their attacks on Garrison, to show his readers how horrendous they were. There was a dialogue within the pages of *The Liberator*, albeit one that was sternly annotated by Garrison, and no one was missing his point.

Though he had a growing number of Boston supporters, Garrison also had many enemies because he insisted that the failure of northern whites to speak out was part of the problem. He singled out the churches for failing to take a moral stance, asserting that there were racist practices even in Boston and that Massachusetts capital, such as textile mills, collaborated with the slave system.

To Garrison, his newspaper was only the beginning. He created the New England Anti-Slavery Society to pull in supporters. They held their first meeting in 1832 during a blustering nor'easter of snow and hail. Attendees included Blacks and whites, aristocrats and middle class. The meeting was in the basement at the First African Meeting House, also known as the First African Baptist Church, on the Black side of Beacon Hill. The church had been founded by Thomas Paul, a Black man from New Hampshire who had been angered by the mistreatment of Blacks at the regular Baptist churches. He founded Black Baptist churches around the country. His son, also named Thomas, was one of Lloyd Garrison's first staff hires for *The Liberator*. Although young Thomas Paul Jr. came from a distinguished family, outsiders criticized Lloyd for spending his meager resources on a Black man. Garrison himself earned $700 a year and, though always in debt, never missed a single week of publication.

In the mid-1820s the First African Meeting House had a Black grammar school in the school room where Garrison had organized the Massachusetts Anti-Slavery Society, and one of their star pupils was William Cooper Nell.

In the mid-1820s there was a citywide examination for grade school students, and the ones with the top results were awarded the Franklin Medal. The recipients received their medals at a dinner given by the aristocratic Mayor Harrison Gray Otis at Faneuil Hall. Nell and two other Black students from his school qualified for the award but were not invited to the mayor's dinner. Instead, they were given vouchers to buy a biography of Benjamin Franklin in a neighborhood bookstore. That was when, at an early age, Nell concluded that segregated schools were not equal.

But Nell was already schooled in political activism. He had friendly relations with Paul and Walker and Garrison, all friends of his politically active parents. His mother, Louisa, worked with the Garrisonians. His father, William, worked closely with Walker in the Massachusetts General Colored Association, founded at the First African Meeting House in 1826. They focused on both ending discrimination in the North and slavery in the South. William Nell demanded the repeal of Massachusetts discriminatory laws, petitioned Congress to end slavery, and published articles in *Freedom's Journal*. The group emphasized organization, and young Nell learned that nothing could be accomplished without organization.

Garrison, through his speeches and his writing style, gained a reputation as a ferocious fanatic, or, as a fellow abolitionist once put it, he was "regarded by some as a monster in human shape." But those who knew him found him warm and affable. He once replied to the accusation that he was dogmatic with "Bow-wow-wow-wow!" He was an incurable punster. He sometimes began a lecture, "Ladies and gentlemen, I am the peace disturber Garrison—the fanatic Garrison—the madman Garrison." Then he would wait a beat until the audience started laughing because this bald man with glasses and a kindly face did not appear to be dangerous.

Garrison was a type of activist until that time seldom seen in America, except possibly for Samuel Adams or Thomas Paine, also an abolitionist. He was a professional agitator. He called his comrades coadjutors.

But in person he was also a jokester who loved a good wisecrack. Harriet Beecher Stowe, the celebrated author of *Uncle Tom's Cabin*, once commented that she thought Garrison was a wolf in sheep's clothing, but once she got to know him, she realized that he was a lamb disguised as a wolf. Emerson once called him "a one-sided man," and it may have been true that Garrison did not approach the issues of the day with the complexity of Emerson, but he did not have a single cause. In addition to abolitionism, he campaigned for temperance, and, with equal forcefulness, for women's rights and for a deep and evolved concept of nonviolence. He also championed Native American and immigrant rights, fought for prison reform, and opposed capital punishment, which he pointed out was used disproportionately for Black people, and he called it "judicial homicide."

James Russell Lowell, one of the most prominent poets of his generation, wrote (and, unsurprisingly, Lloyd Garrison reprinted it in *The Liberator*):

> *There's Garrison, his features very*
> *Benign for an incendiary,*
> *Beaming forth sunshine through his glasses*
> *On the surrounding lads and lasses.*

Photograph of William Cooper Nell.

Three

1833—

HERE I AM!

Who does not see that the American people are over a
subterranean fire, the flames of which are fed by slavery?
—L. Maria Child, *An Appeal in Favor of That*
Class of Americans Called Africans, 1833

F rom the start, Garrison always had the idea that he would build a movement by bringing people in one by one. But he also believed that he could expand his movement more quickly if he had great writers working with him. In 1833, the writer he most wanted, the celebrated L. Maria Child, became committed to the movement.

By then, Garrison had been working for years to bring good writers to his cause. John Greenleaf Whittier, a rural New England poet, grew up on a struggling farm. In the 1820s his sister, Mary, sent his poem "The Deity" to the *Newburyport Press* when Garrison was still working there. Garrison, impressed with not only the writing but also the religious undertone of his poem, took an interest in the young man, who was still a teenager. As a devout Quaker, Whittier was raised with abolitionist ideals. Later, when Garrison was an abolitionist in Boston and Whittier had a growing reputation as a poet and as an abolitionist, Garrison wrote of Whittier to a mutual friend, "Can we not induce him to devote his brilliant genius more to the advancement of our cause?" Lloyd kept talking to the poet, visiting him on his farm in rustic Haverhill, just south of the New Hampshire line.

Garrison also wanted his former employer, David Child, to become part of his team. In the 1820s Child had shown his skills as an editor and writer at the *Massachusetts Journal*. Garrison appreciated David's passion for his ideals, but the two men did not always agree. David was never comfortable with Garrison's rigid belief in nonviolence. And David was not an immediatist, though Lloyd changed his thinking on this. Child turned against colonization, partly because Garrison made him realize that the idea was extremely unpopular in the Black community

Garrison called Child's language "strong and pungent," which was praise from a master. But Garrison had reservations about Child's speaking style. "His voice is harsh and stubborn," Garrison wrote to an associate in Newburyport, "and when exerted, grates painfully upon the ears." But he also said of Child's work on the *Journal*, "He has distinguished himself for his candor, good sense, and sterling independence."

While admiring David, the writer Garrison most wanted to bring to his movement was David's wife, Maria Child. In 1829, Garrison had reprinted some of Maria's writing in Lundy's paper, where he called her "the First woman in the Republic." By this time, this did not seem like an extravagant claim. George Ticknor's backing had established her position.

"No man could consider himself of any account in the world if he was not admitted to Mr. Ticknor's study," quipped Theodore Parker, a fiery transcendentalist minister who was never admitted. Ticknor used his influence to get articles published that praised her lavishly. She had become a star and enjoyed her status. In 1825, Levi Lincoln, the governor of Massachusetts, invited her to a reception, where she met the Marquis de Lafayette. For years after, she maintained that it was one of the high points of her life when the French general kissed her hand.

The same year as the Lafayette kiss, Maria Child's second book, *The Rebels; Or, Boston before the Revolution*, was published and earned even more praise than *Hobomok* and sold out numerous editions. She wrote speeches in her novel and had them delivered by important real-life revolutionaries, and, because of their popularity, these speeches became adopted in school books, without acknowledgment that they were actually fiction. Children even memorized these speeches as part of their schoolwork.

In 1826 she began editing and heavily contributing to the *Juvenal Miscellany*, the first magazine for children in America and possibly the first in the English language. It was filled with poems and stories and games and sometimes only slightly hidden social messages. Children around the country would anxiously await the latest edition.

But while Maria was enjoying great success, David was incurring huge debts, and they were struggling financially. In 1828 two libel cases cost him hundreds of dollars in legal fees. Samuel R. Johnson, a stone cutter and supporter of Andrew Jackson, sued Child for libel when he wrote in the *Massachusetts Journal* that he was bilking the prison system by taking kickbacks for rough stone supplies. He also accused state senator John Keyes of granting printing contracts to the "reprobated Jackson press" without opening other bids. They were in the throes of the bitter 1828 presidential campaign and David Child, who was close to John Quincy Adams and despised Jackson, grew careless in the heat of the moment. He never carefully checked his accusations against these Jacksonians, and he lost both libel cases and was sentenced to six months in prison in 1830. It was reversed on appeal, but by then he had already served the sentence.

David Child was not getting many breaks. The judge in the Keyes case, Marcus Morton, was a strong Jackson supporter. Maria Child was also coming to understand that the great zeal of her husband, for which she admired him, came with a costly carelessness. It was the same impetuousness that had led him to abandon his diplomatic career to fight a hopeless war for the Spanish.

In 1829, she turned her struggles into profit by publishing *The Frugal Housewife*, a book of household advice. All her life, Maria's friends would laugh about her frugality, how she reused envelopes and cut off half pages to use the blank part if the letter was short. Ironically, in private she often expressed how tedious she found household chores. This book on maintaining a household inexpensively was also a cookbook, and while cookbooks by women were enormously popular in the nineteenth century, they were generally for comfortable middle-class people. This was a book for people who, like her, were on a tight budget. She had promised that it would be "suited to the common wants of common people." Apparently, her instincts were correct, because the cookbook went through thirty-three editions in the US, twelve in England, and nine in Germany, and it remains in print today.

Maria Child believed in simplicity: "Eat simple food. Take plenty of exercise. Never fear a little fatigue. Let not children be dressed in tight clothes." She also gave uncomplicated recipes so that a woman would not have to spend her entire day cooking. This was decades ahead of Mrs. Beeton, Fannie Farmer, and other extremely popular cookbook writers for working women at the end of the century.

She gave several recipes for Indian pudding, which remains a uniquely New England classic and, unlike Maria, has absolutely nothing to do with Native Americans. Native Americans were simply the ones who introduced corn to the diet of European Americans, so cornmeal was called Indian meal. It was a dish Maria often served when entertaining fellow abolitionists at her appropriately spare dinner parties.

BAKED INDIAN PUDDING

Indian pudding is good baked. Scald a quart of milk (skimmed milk will do,) and stir in seven table spoonfuls of sifted Indian meal, a tea-spoonful of salt, a tea-cupful of molasses, and a great spoonful of ginger, or sifted cinnamon. Baked three or four hours. If you want whey, you must be sure and pour in a little cold milk, after it is all mixed.

A practiced and gifted writer, Maria created recipes that were not formulaic. A Child recipe or even household advice is conversational. The reader feels as though a friend is talking. This style helped make her work enormously popular, especially

The Frugal Housewife, which unlike most of her other titles, had no political controversy.

By the time David Child was out of prison in 1830, the *Massachusetts Journal* was in serious financial difficulty, and in 1831, it was forced to fold.

In 1832, David and Maria settled into a small house on the Boston waterfront that they called "Le Paradis de Pauvres" ("the poor man's paradise"). She described it as "a very small cottage with a very small garden filled with flowers." She loved gardening. She was charmed by the view, which she sketched—a warehouse on a wharf with barrels and a two-masted ship in the background. They were happy, even as Maria struggled to cover David's debt with her own healthy writing income.

Her successful writing career was their only lifeline and in 1833 she was at her peak. The *North American Review*, which had broken its policy of not reviewing books for children by heaping praise on the *Juvenal Miscellany*, now wrote, "We are not sure that any women of our country could outrank Mrs. Child. . . . Few female writers, if any, have done more or better things for our literature in the lighter or graver departments."

In those early years both Childs were focused on opposing Andrew Jackson and his mistreatment of Native Americans. Lloyd Garrison also championed this cause. In 1824 Garrison wrote a lengthy letter to Jackson, explaining why he was unfit for office and telling him that being a war hero did not qualify him as a candidate for public office. He said that one could

carry out great deeds of bravery in warfare "and yet be dis-
qualified for a civilian as the greatest dunce in Christendom."
Ten years later, William Lloyd Garrison was a well-known
name, but in 1824, Jackson may have wondered who this
Garrison was.

In 1828, Jackson, who was proslavery, defeated Adams, who
opposed slavery, by a landslide. Jackson was everything Garrison
and the Childs feared. In addition to the 1814 Creek War, he
pushed the Seminoles off their land in the 1817 First Seminole
War. Once he became president in 1829 Jackson took on an intense campaign to remove Native Americans from eastern land
with the approval of Congress. The result was the Indian Removal Act of 1830, which forced tens of thousands of Native
Americans off their lands and moved them west of the Mississippi, killing thousands in the process. In 1832 he unleashed the
Second Seminole War, which historians consider the bloodiest
Indian war in American history.

Jackson's persecution of Native Americans was tied to his
support of slavery. Escaped slaves took refuge with the Seminoles and the Seminoles protected them.

In addition to his opposition to Jackson, David Child became
increasingly involved in the abolitionist cause. By 1830, Child
was an early Garrison supporter, one of the first people to whom
Garrison confided his intention to start *The Liberator*. Maria
complained to David that this Garrison, whom she had never
met, was "too ultra, too rash."

But Maria was the writer Garrison dreamed of. Garrison
had David arrange a meeting. Fifty years later at the time of
Garrison's death, she reminisced, "I little thought then that
the whole pattern of my life-web would be changed by that

introduction." She described herself as someone absorbed in poetry and mysticism—"soaring loft, on Psychewings into the ethereal regions of mysticism." (Garrison also wrote poetry and was intrigued by mysticism.) She said of meeting him, "A new stimulus seized my whole being and carried me which so ever it would." Despite this immediate impression, it took about seven months of discussions before Lloyd completely brought Maria around to being a true Garrisonian.

Gradually the influence could be seen. Abolitionist discourse started to seep into her writing. The September/October 1830 issue of the *Juvenal Miscellany* featured "The St. Domingo Orphans," an antislavery story by Maria. From then on she placed antislavery messages in some form in every issue. It was becoming her leading issue, but the public did not have a strong reaction to this. The *Juvenal Miscellany* was a fun and educational publication for children. There was nothing else like it.

Maria Child was still restlessly exploring new forms of writing. In June 1831, she had published *The Mother's Book*, the first in-depth guide to childcare in America, covering everything from infant care to sex education for teenagers. After eight editions, it became the Dr. Spock of its time. This too seemed ironic because, though Maria longed to have a child, she never had one. In hundreds of letters, a yearning for children is expressed but there is no mention of her ever being pregnant.

In 1833 Maria Child executed one of the most spectacular acts of self-destruction in the history of American letters. From her conversations with Garrison Maria began to form an idea for a book—an appeal for abolitionism. Typically, Child backed up her ideas with a great deal of research, and she was able to do this because she had access to the Boston Athenaeum. The

Athenaeum was becoming one of the largest libraries in America. The library, then on Pearl Street, was available to its paid members, but as a special privilege, it offered Maria Child access free of charge; she was only the second woman admitted. There she researched her 1833 book, *An Appeal in Favor of That Class of Americans Called Africans*. The title was a stab at the colonization movement, since Blacks had responded that they were Americans, not Africans.

She spent three years researching this book, not only in the Athenaeum but in a constant dialogue with her husband and Lloyd Garrison and a fastidious reading of every issue of *The Liberator*. Most of the subjects she discussed reflected articles in the Garrison paper. Many of her ideas about the free Black point of view came from published letters from Black readers to *The Liberator*. Writings in *The Liberator* were her first contacts with Black people. At the time, Garrison was one of the few white Bostonians who actually met with and spoke with Black people. *An Appeal* was the first textbook of abolitionism ever written, and it was largely Garrisonian abolitionism but written in a softer tone than Garrison's. It became the foremost treatise on the abolitionist cause.

In this book, Maria Child did not simply lecture southern slave owners on the immorality of slavery; she argued that it was against the best interest of their society. She noted that slavery created a white class that was unproductive, leading to "indolence," and she provided ample evidence that slave plantations misused and exhausted the soil so that plantations were in constant search of new fields. She suggested that this was why slave owners needed to expand slavery into new territories, maintaining a completely inefficient economic system.

Child's publisher, Ticknor and Allen, was new and not afraid of controversy. They had only started publishing the year before out of the Old Corner Bookstore in downtown Boston at Washington and School Streets. The publisher, William Davis Ticknor, only twenty-two years old at the time, was a cousin of George Ticknor. William Ticknor changed partners the next year, becoming Ticknor and Fields, soon one of the most important publishers in America. They remained Maria Child's publisher and featured other important New England abolitionists on their list, including James Russell Lowell, John Greenleaf Whittier, and Harriet Beecher Stowe. They were also printers of the *North American Review* and they published Hawthorne, Emerson, Thoreau, Henry Wadsworth Longfellow, and other luminaries.

But on their distinguished list there was no book as controversial as Maria Child's *An Appeal*. The window of the Old Corner Bookstore was smashed by an angry reader because Child's book was on display. Some, such as the manager of the American Bible Society, refused to read it because it was said that reading this book would turn you into an abolitionist. Child was not surprised by the angry response to her book. In the opening pages, she wrote, "I am fully aware of the unpopularity of the task I have undertaken; but though I expect ridicule and censure, I cannot fear them."

The anger came not only from the South. She infuriated northerners by suggesting that they showed even greater racial prejudice than southerners. She specifically impugned New Englanders, who had always felt above the fray. She hoped to shatter this complacency.

A few weeks after publication Child received a note from the Athenaeum saying that the trustees had decided to revoke her privileges.

In fact, her entire career seemed to be mysteriously evaporating like a puddle on hot pavement. Only a month after being anointed the leading woman writer in the *North American Review*, and despite being published by his cousin William, George Ticknor and his aristocratic circle abruptly blackballed her and would turn icily away if they saw her on the street. They even shunned anyone who did not snub her. James T. Austin, a future Massachusetts Attorney General, picked up the book with a pair of tongs and tossed it out a window. Wealthy Bostonians earned their living from slavery, shipping, sugar refining, and textile mills. To them, abolition was a threat. Maria was exposing them on this very point.

Sales of *The Frugal Housewife* plunged. Subscribers vanished from The *Juvenile Miscellany* and the magazine was forced to close. Parents did not want their children exposed to the writings of a radical. Most of Child's other books went out of print. Even family members turned on her. Her brother, James, who had named a daughter Lydia Maria and another after the lead character in *Hobomok*, became openly antagonistic. Twisted by a hatred that did not come from his family, he denounced "niggers" and "nigger lovers." Old friends, such as Lois Curtis, in whose home David had proposed to Maria, turned against her.

In 1839 Harriet Martineau, a British writer and reportedly the first female sociologist, was inspired to write an article after a trip to Boston called "The Martyr Age in America." In it, she described Maria Child as "a lady of whom society was extremely proud before she published her *Appeal*, and to whom society has been extremely contemptuous ever since."

But not everyone felt that way. In an age when women did not participate in political movements, Maria Child became recognized as a leader of the abolitionists. In 1831 and 1832,

Garrisonians had become increasingly organized, and David and Maria often came to meetings. By 1833, she was recognized as one of them, and Garrison's inner circle was ecstatic about her book. Unitarian minister Samuel May, to whom the book was dedicated, wrote, "That such an author—ay, such an *authority*—should espouse our cause . . . , was a matter of no small joy." Looking back, he said, "We had seen her often at our meetings. We knew that she sympathized with her brave husband in his abhorrence of our American system of slavery; but we did not know that she had so carefully studied and thoroughly mastered the subject."

Many of the pivotal Boston abolitionists were brought to the cause after reading Maria Child's book. The outspoken Thomas Wentworth Higginson, an athletic Harvard-educated minister who had lost his congregation for preaching radical ideas against slavery, wrote, "I know that, on reading it for the first time, nearly ten years after its first appearance, it had more formative influence on my mind in that direction than any other."

Boston-born Charles Sumner, though his father had been an abolitionist, said that he solidified his abolitionist convictions when he read Child's book. And then he became a pivotal figure in the abolitionist movement.

Some abolitionists of a more conservative bent worried that Maria Child had gone too far. William Ellery Channing, a leading Unitarian minister and a moderate abolitionist, hiked the winding streets of Boston for more than a mile from Beacon Hill to the Childs' cottage by the harbor. He wanted to talk to Maria about her book. While there was much he admired about the book and its research, he said that she had become too much of a "zealot." Maria made it her goal to bring Channing around.

Many of what was becoming Garrison's inner circle—the Lorings, Maria Chapman and her husband, and the Sewalls—attended Channing's church. Maria Child, according to her letters, made little progress with Channing on the first meeting, but they met regularly, and in time, the minister became as much a zealot as she was.

She was a challenge to other writers who harbored abolitionist sentiments. John Greenleaf Whittier took note of Maria, and the same year *An Appeal* was published, perhaps inspired by her, he decided to put aside his growing literary career to dedicate himself to the cause of abolition. He described this decision and announced his new position:

> *"Forego thy dreams of lettered ease,*
> *Put thou the scholar's promise by.*
> *The rights of man are more than these."*
> *He heard and answered: "Here am I!"*

Friends and associates commented on the tremendous sacrifice Maria Child had made for the cause. With admiration, aristocratic Wendell Phillips wrote, "Hardly ever was there a costlier sacrifice.... Narrow means just changing to ease; after a weary struggle, fame and social position in her grasp; every door opening before her; the sweetness of having her genius recognized."

But she never spoke that way. In the mountain of letters she wrote to friends and relatives she never expressed regret. She did occasionally comment that she had planned to live the life of a writer and not an activist. She wrote Higginson, "My natural inclinations drew me much more strongly towards literature and the arts than towards reform, and the weight of conscience was needed to turn the scale."

It was not the life she wanted, but she had no choice. She was always driven by her conscience and the few times in her life when she attempted to withdraw from activism, her conscience pulled her back. In 1833 she had made a choice. Her goal was to end slavery, a true immediatist. She wrote in the preface of *An Appeal*, "Should it be the means of advancing, even one single hour, the inevitable progress of truth and justice, I would not exchange the consciousness for all the Rothchilds' wealth or Sir Walter's fame." She changed her life and looked to a new role in the world and was eager to work with a new and growing set of colleagues.

They were a small group tightly knit by deep convictions. They rejoiced every time a recruit would be convinced to call himself or herself an abolitionist. The small Boston Clique was growing in both Black and white communities. Thomas Paul's African Meeting House on Beacon Hill also had an abolitionist clique and the two often worked together, the Garrisonians visiting Beacon Hill and the Beacon Hill activists visiting the downtown parlor.

In 1833 at the age of sixteen, William Cooper Nell made his first speech at the Juvenile Garrison Independent Society, which met at the African Meeting House. He said that the key was organizing "by uniting together and assisting each other—you will soon have the satisfaction of knowing that the oppressed are enabled to exclaim, 'WE ARE FREE!!'" It was also his first of many speeches denouncing segregated schools.

He began working for Garrison at *The Liberator* and learned the skills needed to publish a journal.

For a time, he wanted to be a lawyer. Like David Child, and many who go to law school, he thought the law was a great tool for political activism. He studied law under the abolitionist lawyer William Bowditch, who helped move refugees in the Underground Railroad. Nell decided not to become a lawyer when Wendell Phillips, also a lawyer, pointed out that it required an oath swearing to defend the Constitution, which accepted the legality of slavery. His teacher Bowditch always said that when one's conscience conflicted with the law, the law should be disobeyed. In 1846 Bowditch resigned his commission as justice of the peace because it required an oath swearing to support the Constitution.

Centered around the force of Lloyd Garrison's personality, Maria Child's book had laid a foundation. In the 1850s, she wrote to Whittier recalling 1833 as "those noble self-forgetting days." She did not miss her old world, "the constrained elegancies of Beacon Street." She wrote that abolitionism had brought her "to the noblest and best of the land, intellectually and morally, and knit us together in that firm friendship which grows out of sympathy in a good but unpopular cause."

The Garrisonians wanted more than just building a tight little group in Boston, though that was also hard work. The larger goal was to build a national movement, to turn the country against slavery, to make slavery no longer acceptable to the American people. The idea of abolition was catching on. Abolitionists were becoming known and imitated throughout the country. By 1833 there were forty-seven abolitionist societies in ten of the fourteen northern states. The Garrisonians sensed that the movement was growing. It was, at least, a beginning.

Daguerreotype of Maria Weston Chapman, 1846.

Four

1835—

SISTERS IN THE CLIQUE

When Bonaparte told a French lady that he did not like to hear a woman talk politics, she replied,—"Sire, in a country where women are beheaded, it is very natural that they should like to know the reason." And where women are brutalized, scourged, and sold, shall we not inquire the reason?

—Lydia Maria Child, *Rights and Wrongs in Boston*, 1836

By 1835 Maria Child was one of several women of prominence in the abolitionist movement, and soon others joined. This in itself was a growing controversy in a society where women were not expected to be involved in politics.

The initial fight was over immediatism, but the Garrisonians had considerable success convincing would-be abolitionists that emancipation should be immediate. This had become a widespread definition of abolitionism. The Garrisonians had also convinced many abolitionists that the freed Blacks should have full rights of citizenship. Not everyone agreed, though, and there were other controversies simmering. Typical of a growing movement, new ideas and new controversies appeared regularly.

A key figure in this movement was David Child, who, though penniless and out of work, was at the height of his reputation among abolitionists as the fearless fighter who dared the impossible. David was bold and never hesitated. Along with Samuel Sewall, his Harvard classmate, he founded an integrated college, the Noyes Academy, committed to treating Black and white students equally. At the time, there were no Black colleges in America. And only a few Black students were admitted to colleges. The first Black student to graduate from any college was in 1823 from Middlebury College in Vermont. Ten years later, it was still a rare occurrence.

The Noyes Academy was to change this. David Child promised to teach there and, though he was preoccupied with a law case in Boston at the time of the school's opening, probably would have come later if the school had lasted.

Citizens of Canaan, New Hampshire, the town where the school was established, became obsessed with the idea that they were about to be overrun by Black people, who they claimed were lawless and dangerous. Shortly after the school opened in 1835, three hundred townspeople calling themselves "patriots in the spirit of '75" (violence was often justified by the Revolution), with one hundred yoke of oxen, tore the building down and dragged it into a nearby swamp. Ironic that they thought Black people were lawless.

Child was by now developing a skill for bouncing back from calamity and was respected in the Garrison group for his persistence. Garrison regularly expressed admiration for him. In 1835 David Child was elected Vice President of the Massachusetts Anti-Slavery Society (a newer version of the New England Anti-Slavery Society) and was also nominated for the US Senate in an unsuccessful bid to place an abolitionist in the chamber.

Who better than David Child to put up for a losing cause? In 1835 there were still many voters for whom *abolitionist* was a *dirty* word. There was clearly not enough support to elect a committed abolitionist to the Senate. The certainty that he would not be elected may explain why Garrison backed Child's candidacy and even wrote in *The Liberator* about what a fine senator he would make, which might have been true. But Garrison adamantly opposed abolitionists serving in public office and participating in the criminal government.

For David Child, who always harbored political ambitions, this would become a thorny point of disagreement. Many other abolitionists also opposed Garrison's position. The abolitionists were gaining strength. In 1835 elected office for abolitionists was not yet possible, but in time it would be. It is not known if David Child thought he could win in 1835, but his defeat was a disappointment. By the time abolitionists had a chance at winning such races, they had lost confidence in Child, who had seen too many failures.

The Boston abolitionists did not look like most political movements of the early nineteenth century. Not only were there prominent Black activists, mostly from Boston's free Black population, but there were also outspoken women participating.

The issue of women's rights had been smoldering in New England for some time. Abigail Adams, John Adams's wife, was one of the early New England feminists. She argued to her husband that women should participate in the Continental Congress and that they should be given a part in the new government that was being created. In March 1776, in a letter to her husband, she wrote, "I desire you would remember the ladies and be more generous and favorable to them than your ancestors." She also had strong abolitionist sentiments and protested when the anti-slavery passage of the Declaration of Independence written by Jefferson was removed from the document as too controversial.

Lloyd Garrison believed that women should have the same rights as men and was eager to have women participate as full members in his movement. *The Liberator* had a "Ladies Department" that attempted to stir outrage by describing the brutal treatment of enslaved women, calling on women to rise up to defend their sisters. A notable number did. Ads for the Massachusetts Anti-Slavery Society's monthly meeting noted, "Ladies are particularly invited to be present." Women abolitionists, including Maria Child, drew parallels between the denial of rights to Black people and the oppression of women in general. They also pointed out, as did Garrison, that women slaves were beaten, raped, forced to produce children, and had their children taken away from them. Women asserted (and many men did too) that slavery was a crime against women.

In 1833, the year of Maria Child's *Appeal*, Lloyd Garrison spent time in England. The British had just abolished slavery. He found that women had played an important role, collecting eight hundred thousand signatures on petitions to Parliament. He returned to the US convinced that American women would be crucial to his movement as well. "We cannot believe that our ladies are less philanthropic or less influential," he wrote in *The Liberator*. In a society in which women could not vote, their public speaking was frowned upon, and they were told not to engage in politics, many women were central figures in the Garrison movement. Their participation was not without controversy. One of the differences between the Garrison group and the Quakers was that once the Quakers ruled on something, every Quaker had to follow it or leave the community. Garrison had many ideas and beliefs, but only one was required to be part of his group: support for the immediate abolition of slavery. Some of his followers were even a little indecisive about that.

This openness was Garrison's strength. It enabled him to run a movement of freethinkers and open discussion, the kind of society he believed in. His famous dictum, "I will be heard!" never precluded a willingness to listen, consider, and discuss. Some of his editorials in *The Liberator* invited those of different opinions to write in. This habit of open exchanges gave him the ability to work with abolitionist societies with whom he did not agree in New York, Ohio, and other states. It also meant bringing in people who had differences but were loyal to the cause such as David Child, and some of whom could later be persuaded, such as the Reverend Channing.

Many abolitionists did not approve of the way women participated in Garrison's movement and especially opposed them giving public speeches. One of the many reasons some Bostonians had such disdain for Maria Child's *Appeal* was that they believed it was not a woman's place to be speaking out on such issues. The *North American Review*, her former champion, denounced her for entering the world of male politics.

In fact, even though they made Maria Child's *Appeal* required reading for its members, the American Anti-Slavery Society, a New York group that aspired to a nationwide membership, did not allow female members. A number of Quaker women stubbornly participated anyway. Women were allowed to speak in Quaker meetings and so the Quakers produced women with practiced speaking skills, such as Nantucket-born Lucretia Mott. Mott and other Quaker women not only spoke at Quaker meetings but insisted on speaking at abolitionist organizations such as Garrison's Massachusetts Anti-Slavery Society.

For a Quaker to oppose slavery was normal, but for some, like Lucretia Mott, it became a consuming passion. One of the women Garrison brought into the movement was Susan B. Anthony. Her father was a Quaker but her mother came from a family that had fought in the Revolution. Both parents had strong abolitionist convictions. Her parents introduced Susan to Lloyd Garrison and, after lengthy conversations, she too became a committed abolitionist. Most of her seven siblings were also active abolitionists.

As abolitionism grew, an increasing number of women assumed important roles. Tall, statuesque, with striking blue eyes, curly blond hair, a silken voice, and a stately charisma, Maria Weston Chapman looked like she belonged in Ticknor's crowd—the Boston ideal of a female aristocrat. Maria Child later said of her first impression, "We thought her a spy or maybe a slave holder." But she became instead a mainstay of the Garrison group.

In 1830 Maria Weston had married Henry Chapman, an affluent Boston merchant and regular contributor to the cause. In 1833, with twelve other women, including her three sisters, and Louisa Nell, mother of William Cooper Nell, Maria Weston Chapman formed the Boston Female Anti-Slavery Society. They met once a week, distributed *The Liberator*, and collected signatures for petitions to abolish slavery that were sent to Washington.

This group worked to bring in other women, but Maria Child did not want to join. Always extremely protective of her independence, Child never liked to join organizations. But she also questioned the idea of a women's organization, believing women should take their place in what had previously been exclusive to men. In 1839, in a letter to Lucretia Mott, who had become a close friend, she wrote of women's organizations, "They always seemed to me like half a pair of scissors."

Maria Child never became comfortable with public speaking, not because she opposed women speaking, but because she didn't like that kind of public role, preferring to be a writer and advisor. She had close ties to the other women, but she mainly attended Garrison's meetings and would not speak. Lucretia Mott, on the other hand, was a great speaker, and spoke at both women's and men's organizations. Garrison welcomed her oratory gifts. But, the opposite of Maria Child, Mott hated writing.

Maria Child wanted to write a large history of the status of women around the world. It was the kind of book she could have researched at the Athanaeum, but now, cut off from that library, she needed funds for books and research, and she and David had no money. Maria Chapman started selling shares at $100 each for the project. In 1835 Maria Child published her two-volume *History of the Condition of Women*, and it became a reference book for the authors of major feminist works that followed.

Lloyd Garrison was pleased to have the support of women, either in their own organization or in his. He considered Maria Chapman his number-one lieutenant. She edited *The Liberator* when Garrison was traveling. Samuel May said the two Marias—Chapman and Child—were "in a private way . . . the presiding geniuses in all our councils and public meetings, often proposing the wisest measures and suggesting the most weighty thoughts, pertinent facts and apt illustrations."

Much of this counseling took place in the Chapmans' parlor, where the group started to be referred to as "the Boston Clique." The Chapmans lived near the Garrisons, as did Ellis Gray Loring and his wife Louisa. Both Childs and Samuel Sewall and Maria Chapman's sisters, Caroline and Anne, were also usually there.

The Boston Clique were literally teetotalers. Some, like Garrison, were active temperance campaigners. At the Chapmans' they always sipped tea while discussing strategies. It was a small core group, but anyone with an idea could drop by to discuss it. The Chapman parlor was where activists were found plotting for the movement. If local free Blacks wanted to discuss action against discrimination in Boston, if abolitionists from other parts of New England or even other parts of the country wanted to discuss closer coordination with Boston and Garrison, this was the place to go. It was described by Garrison to his wife Helen in an 1836 letter:

> *In the evening I took tea at Mrs. Chapman's; after which, as I sat holding a brisk conversation with the Westons and Chapmans, who should come into the room with bro. May, but our esteemed friend Wm. Goodell from Providence?*

When the Grimké sisters, Angelina and Sarah, abandoned their slaveholding family in South Carolina and moved to the North to work for abolition, they went to Boston and spoke about ideas at the Chapman parlor, which Angelina described as "a conclave of brothers and sisters who all believed a new order of things is very desirable." They were curiosities not only because they were women speakers but because they were southerners with a slaveholding background. They knew the adversaries and they drew enormous crowds.

Abby Kelley was a Quaker who began reading *The Liberator* when she was a schoolteacher in Lynn, Massachusetts. She joined the local women's antislavery society in 1835. By 1838 she had given up teaching to be a full-time activist. Some, it was said, came to her events for the curiosity of seeing a woman speaker, rare among nineteenth-century women, but not unusual for Boston abolitionists. She gave speeches in which she denounced the traditional marriage in which wives were kept "like dolls in a parlor." In one speech to a women's group she stated, "Women revolt at the idea of marrying for the sake of a home, for the sake of a support—of marrying the purse instead of the man. There is no woman here, who, if the question were put to her, would not say, Love is sufficient."

Influenced by Angelina Grimké, who led her to Garrison, Abby Kelley became one of the most militant Garrisonians, demanding immediate emancipation, and full rights for Blacks and embracing Garrison's strict code of nonviolence, including rejection of any role in government. Speaking extemporaneously, in the Quaker style, she could rally people to the cause. She was said to be an attractive woman, although she always dressed plainly in Quaker gray. She could bring audiences to tears with stories of slave children taken from their mothers or tales of women beaten and otherwise abused. Lloyd Garrison described her as "most persevering, most self-sacrificing, most energetic, most meritorious of coadjutors."

Abby traveled the northern states speaking. She raised money from local abolitionists, found staff, and started antislavery newspapers.. She regularly reported back to Boston on how best to reach people in the hinterlands. It was dangerous work, but though she was jeered at and sometimes had rocks thrown at her, she was unstoppable.

In Boston, abolitionism became an interracial movement. And if it was shocking for white women to be publicly addressing political issues, it was even more shocking that in Boston, Black women were also speaking out with great skill and force.

Before the famous white Garrisonian women—before Child and Chapman—was Maria Stewart. Born in Hartford, Connecticut, she was orphaned as a child and made her way as a domestic servant. She moved to Boston in 1826 and married a successful fitter of fishing and whaling vessels. They were part of a small group of Boston middle-class Blacks. When Lloyd Garrison called for the contribution of women in 1831, Maria Stewart came to *The Liberator* with an essay, which Garrison immediately published. She called for Black unity and for Blacks to organize not only against slavery but also against racism in the North. She called for the free Blacks of Boston to organize against local racism. She also decried the oppression of women by both white and Black men.

Soon she began giving speeches—the first American woman to give speeches to gender-mixed audiences and the first Black woman to lecture on abolition and women's rights. In September 1832, she delivered a talk in Franklin Hall to both men and women, declaring that the African Americans of Boston were scarcely better off than southern slaves. She urged Blacks to be more politically active. "Why sit ye here and die?" In February 1833, she gave a speech at the African Masonic Hall in which she derided Black men for not accomplishing more.

Maria Child wrote in her *Appeal*, "The market is so glutted with flattery, that a little truth might be acceptable, were it only for its rarity." But Maria Stewart's candor was not appreciated in Boston. She was denounced in print and by angry crowds on the street. She soon withdrew to New York, where she traded activism for teaching.

In Boston her role was soon filled by Susan Paul, daughter of Garrison's friend, the Baptist minister Thomas Paul, and sister to Garrison's early employee, Thomas Paul Jr.

Susan's father introduced Susan to Maria Child. They both saw themselves as artists—Maria the writer and Susan the musician—and they became close friends. In her early twenties, Susan joined the New England Anti-Slavery Society.

A schoolteacher, Susan Paul was also a gifted singer who gave classical performances on Beacon Hill. She was active in the temperance movement, which brought her closer to Garrison. Susan organized a choir of young Black singers, the Garrison Juvenile Choir, which sang at abolitionist meetings and other events, inspiring crowds with abolitionist and anti-colonization songs, what later would be called "freedom songs."

In 1835 Susan Paul published *Memoir of James Jackson* about her six-year-old student who had died. It was the first-ever biography about an African American. Susan became a vice president of the second Anti-Slavery Convention of American Women and a close advisor to Lloyd Garrison on the subject of women's rights. And then, just when she was becoming a leading figure, in 1841, at the age of thirty-two, she died of tuberculosis.

Among the most prominent Black abolitionists were Sarah Parker Remond and Charles Lenox Remond, sister and brother from Salem. Their father was a barber who immigrated from Curaçao. The Remonds had eight children, most of whom worked in the family catering business and chain of hair salons. Both Sarah and Charles were prominent speakers on the abolitionist circuit. Charles Remond is said to have been the first Black person to give a public speech on abolition. He was close to Garrison and in 1840, the two traveled together to an international antislavery convention in London, where they were welcomed as the leading voices of American abolitionism.

The Boston Clique had a gentility, in part from its being centered on married couples who worked together. But while most in the Clique, like David and Maria Child or the Weston-Chapmans, had marriages in which husband and wife were equal partners in political activism, Lloyd Garrison had a more conventional marriage.

Before marriage, he seemed to live a lonely life. He was warmly greeted at regular events in the Black community, especially at Paul's African Meeting House. Garrison was one of the first white Bostonians to socialize with Black people. He also ate stew and Indian pudding with the Childs at their cottage and sipped tea in the Chapmans' parlor. He supported himself with odd jobs. But with no love life or family life, he had taken to writing poetry and much of it was about unrequited love. Approaching the age of thirty, he was a single man surrounded by married couples.

In 1834 he met Helen Benson. "If it was not love at first sight, it was something very like it," he later wrote. Helen was the daughter of George Benson, a leading abolitionist in Rhode Island. Lloyd was her hero. She wrote him, "How little do I merit so much affection from so noble a being, but as it is offered in sincerity, I will accept it all and confide in your kind and gentle love." They wrote such love letters regularly, back and forth, for eight months, and then, in September 1834, they married.

This was not like the Childs, a marriage of equal partners working together for the cause. Garrison was concerned about supporting his wife and even considered closing down *The Liberator* to concentrate on something more profitable. But Helen would not consider such a sacrifice. She would take charge of domestic life and leave her husband free to focus on his important work. She also hosted. The Boston Clique sometimes met for tea at the Garrison downtown home. When they moved to 65 Suffolk Street (today Shawmut Avenue), the room was called "Helen's Parlor."

Lloyd was an active father who played with his children and rummaged through the kitchen pots and pans to make them dinner during abolitionist meetings. They had seven children, two of whom died in infancy. All of his children except his daughter Helen were named after contemporary abolitionists, including Wendell Phillips Garrison and George Thompson Garrison. They were all raised to be abolitionists. Helen recalled her father tucking her in at night by saying, "What a nice warm bed my darling has. The poor little slave child is not so fortunate and is torn from its mother's arms." When her hands were cold, he told her to warm them on his bald head, which he said was "incendiary." This was typical Garrison humor (southern slave owners often said that he was incendiary and caused slave rebellions).

When the abolitionists decided to bombard Washington with petitions to end slavery, borrowing an idea from the British, women went door to door gathering signatures. Usually, these petitions had twice as many women's signatures as those of men. Women abolitionists were often successful fundraisers. They produced clothing and other items to sell. They sold subscriptions to abolitionist publications.

In 1834 Maria Child and Louisa Loring organized a fair in the Massachusetts Anti-Slavery Society office at 46 Washington Street in downtown Boston. Louisa provided the funds and Maria collected the goods. The hall was decorated with such slogans as "Remember those in bonds, as though bound with them." A plate of cookies had a sign: "Sugar not made by slaves." They sold other free-labor sugar products. They also sold books, handicrafts, and clothing. That fair raised between two hundred and three hundred dollars.

The following year, Maria Chapman took over and turned it into a more profitable annual event. Instead of the quaint items gathered for the first fair, she solicited valuable antiques and works of art. English sympathizers sent fine tea sets. There were also products from New England, such as shells and coral from the Sandwich Islands, contributed by friends in Nantucket, and the famous baskets from Salem. Maria Child, Louisa Nell, and many other women abolitionists worked hard at this annual fair. They hosted the fair in a larger space, Marlborough Hall, and decorated it for the season with evergreens and banners with abolitionist slogans. By the 1840s and into the 1850s, it was a major Boston event at the start of the holiday season, bringing in more than $4,000 each year. Maria Chapman, the grand dame, would buzz from table to table, keeping everything in order.

James Russell Lowell describes Maria Chapman at the 1846 fair:

The coiled-up mainspring of the Fair,
Originating everywhere.
The expansive force, without a sound,
That whirls a hundred wheels around. . . .

While women eagerly engaged in such traditional female activities, many sought a far greater role in the movement. Most of the women abolitionists such as Maria Child, Abby Kelley, Maria Chapman, Susan Paul, Louisa Nell, Lucretia Mott, and Susan B. Anthony were what today would be called militant feminists. How could you champion the rights of some and not others? How could women fight for the rights of Blacks to vote when they didn't have that right? How could you fight for the full rights of citizenship for Black men and not Black women?

Abolitionism showed women how to build a movement. Women's suffrage sprang from the abolitionist movement in the same way the so-called "second wave" of women's rights sprang from the Civil Rights movement in the 1960s.

Many Boston abolitionist men, too, actively supported women's rights, including the right to vote. Emerson and the transcendentalists were also supporters of women's rights. The rights of women was one of the most divisive controversies in abolitionism, something that drove some away from Garrison. Many of Garrison's inner circle, including such loyalists as Whittier, did not oppose women's rights but thought it deflected from the main issue of abolition and was draining support. They thought Garrison was weakening their antislavery cause by bringing in other issues and he took on too many issues—women's rights, nonviolence, prison reform, temperance, and more. But to Garrison, the liberation of Black people and the liberation of women were the same issue. He argued that when the injustice of slavery was closely examined, many related ills in society were revealed.

By the late 1830s, a split on the women's rights issue among abolitionists was becoming apparent. The Massachusetts Anti-Slavery Society and the New England Anti-Slavery Convention in 1837 had welcomed women as voting members. But in New York, the American Anti-Slavery Society had not ruled on the issue. In 1839 New England women were determined to have full participation at the big AASS meeting in New York.

Horace Moulton, a Massachusetts Methodist minister and devoted abolitionist, said that he was "sickened" to see that the Massachusetts society was sending women as delegates. "I am for having women enjoy their rights, but do not wish to have them claim the prerogatives of men." Elizur Wright, who had turned to immediatism after reading Lloyd Garrison's pamphlet on the subject and was one of the founders of the AASS, said that he was "opposed to hens crowing." But Wright also believed it would be destructive to the movement to attempt to bar the women delegates. After a two-day debate, it was decided to seat the women, which led to some withdrawals from the organization. Whittier was right in fearing that women's issues would drive some away. But supporting women's rights remained at the core of the Boston Clique. Abolitionism was growing in popularity across the northern states, especially in the West—Ohio, Indiana, Illinois, and the new state of Michigan. As the number of militants grew, it was becoming more difficult to speak in one voice from Boston. More divisive issues were to come.

Adin Ballou.

Five

1837—
THE MOST DIFFICULT
PRINCIPLE

Men have become drunk with mutual revenge; and
they who could inflict the greatest amount of injury, in
pretended defense of life, honor, rights, and property,
institutions, and laws, have been idolized as the heroes
and rightful sovereigns of the world. Non-resistance
explodes this horrible delusion.

—Adin Ballou, *Christian Non-Resistance*
in All Its Important Bearings, 1845

In the mid-1830s, violence against abolitionists was steadily
increasing, and at the same time, the abolitionists' belief in
nonviolence was taking root. Advocates of nonviolence were
regularly being tested. Abolitionists were being attacked by violent mobs—"the mobocracy," it was called—and they refused to
fight back. But a showdown was inevitable and nonviolence would

reach a defining test in 1837 when slavers attacked an abolitionist who, unlike the ones before him, took up arms against his assailants. He was killed and the question became whether to praise or rebuke his actions. Was he a martyr or had he betrayed their principles? Would they have the courage to denounce someone fighting for their cause? They would have to face this thoughtfully in 1837 because this polemic was certain to arise again.

By 1837 abolitionists had been braced for this for a number of years. In 1835, herded through the streets of Boston by an angry mob, with a rope tied around him, keeping his dignity and not fighting them off, William Lloyd Garrison bravely showed the public what nonresistance was about. He showed how an abolitionist should face a mob. It left a lasting impression and strengthened the cause of nonresistance.

Nonresistance, the term that was used at the time, came from Matthew 5:39, "Resist not evil." The term was as misleading as the word pacifism. It was not about not resisting. A pacifist is an activist. A nonresistant resists. But they believed the resistance must be accomplished in a way that does not harm the adversary. The question became: how to effect change, how to stave off a violent adversary, how to resist aggression, without a violent response? By 1835 many abolitionists, such as Abby Kelley, had turned their cheek to violent attacks.

Lloyd Garrison and many of the nonresistants of early nineteenth-century New England had their roots in what was called "the Great Awakening." After the religious fervor of the Puritans faded, there was, in the mid-eighteenth century, a new revival of religious zeal that emphasized the individual's covenant with God. Its impact was felt during the American Revolution.

The Awakening condemned existing social orders as depraved. It emphasized the idea that America had a special mission to build Christ's kingdom. The Revolution was the first step. The new generation—people such as Lloyd Garrison and David Child—still believed in this special mission and found that America was failing to achieve its destiny.

From this movement, the Awakening, came the idea that an individual should be a reformer. As Emerson, with his transcendental philosophy, put it in an 1841 essay, "What is man born for but to be a reformer, a remaker of what man has made; a renouncer of lies."

This thinking was not only at the root of transcendentalism; it was fundamental to Garrisonian abolitionism. Lloyd Garrison saw himself as a reformer. He also embraced another idea that came from the Awakening, "perfectionism"—the idea that God on earth could be obtained if an individual strived to be perfect. This was why Garrison was not concerned about whether his coadjutors shared all his beliefs; he had to do what he believed was right, and if he did, the world would change. He wrote:

> *"Instead, therefore, of assailing the doctrine, 'Be ye perfect, even as your Father in Heaven is perfect,' let us all aim to establish it, not merely as theoretical right, but as practically attainable."*

He saw nonresistance as the first step toward "God on earth." This meant following the teachings of Christ to love your enemy, do no harm to anyone, and forgive those who try to harm you. If someone does evil, one accomplishes nothing by responding with more evil. Otherwise it becomes what peace resister Adin Ballou called "mutual revenge."

For several years, Garrison refused to appear for obligatory training with the Massachusetts militia, a standard requirement in most states in the early nineteenth century. His nearsightedness would have made him ineligible, but he also refused to present a certificate of his disability. In 1829 he was ordered to pay a fine, which he did. Ever after, he told conscientious objectors that a nonresistant should pay the fine. This was a moral and not a monetary issue.

From the outset Garrison made nonresistance central to his movement. His original 1831 statement of principles in *The Liberator* declared, "War . . . whether offensive or defensive, is contrary to the precepts and example of Christ."

As the movement was assembled in the early 1830s, Garrisonians were committed to ending slavery without violence. Their alternative weapon was what they called "moral suasion." Emerson, who generally agreed with Garrison but found "the one-sided man" too simplistic, had his own variation on moral suasion. He believed the solution was to buy all the slaves from the slave owners, convincing slave owners that slavery was morally wrong, deteriorated society, and was even harmful to agriculture. A few southerners had seen this. Even Thomas Jefferson in his racist 1784 *Notes on the State of Virginia* wrote, "There must, doubtless, be an unhappy influence on the manners of the people, produced by the existence of slavery among us."

Moral suasion was not a lofty, remote idea in an age that celebrated the importance of reason for resolving issues. Reason was central to the ideas of eighteenth-century thinkers. Jean-

Jacques Rousseau, the French philosopher who was one of Jefferson's inspirations, wrote about the importance of reason in reaching a just society. One of Thomas Paine's famous pamphlets had the title *The Age of Reason*, and it argued for reason as the way to arrive at truth. Immanuel Kant, the influential German philosopher, wrote, "All our knowledge begins with the senses, proceeds then to the understanding, and ends with reason. There is nothing higher than reason."

John Adams was typical of his age. He believed in reason, in moral suasion, and also in warfare. Years after the Revolutionary War, he stated that the Revolution had been accomplished before the war began; he said this had been accomplished by a change "in the mind and hearts of the people." To Massachusetts abolitionists, Adams was the most important Founding Father. He had said that the Revolution would not be finished until slavery was ended. He was the leader of an essentially nonviolent movement with tactics of nonviolent noncooperation until the 1775 battles of Lexington and Concord began a shooting war.

It is an important lesson that once those guns were fired, nonviolent approaches were no longer possible. Adams had argued that although much had been accomplished through civil disobedience, only a war—only violence—could truly forge a nation. This was an enduring way of thinking that Garrisonians were always fighting. A century after Adams, Karl Marx famously asserted the same idea based on what he had learned from studying both the American and French Revolutions. "Violence is the midwife of history," he concluded. He maintained that without violence nothing changes.

But to Garrison, violence was where history went wrong.

Change would only be effective if it were accomplished without violence and instead by changing minds. Reason. The fact that abolitionists had succeeded in England in 1833, without force, proved his theory. But there were important differences. British slavery was in their distant colonies, not in the country itself, and the slave sugar plantations were failing economically. That might have happened in the United States, but cotton had become hugely profitable. It is always difficult to argue against something that makes a lot of money.

To Garrisonians, moral suasion was the only way to triumph over slavery. Garrison wrote, "The history of mankind is crowded with evidence proving that physical coercion is not adapted to moral regeneration." Abolition agents were sent far and wide to persuade, circulating pamphlets and books. This was why Lloyd wanted writers on his team.

In the 1820s and '30s, peace movements were fashionable in America as a reaction to the War of 1812 and in Europe in response to the Napoleonic Wars. In 1826 Lloyd met William Ladd, a burly, good-natured man who had graduated from Harvard and then gone to sea. His father was a wealthy merchant, and he became captain of one of his father's ships and earned a reputation as a hard-drinking, skilled sea captain. Then he operated a cotton plantation in Florida, refusing to use slaves and hiring European immigrants. The plantation failed. In his late thirties, about 1816, he embraced Christianity. He gave up drinking and smoking, got a license to preach, and traveled New England talking about nonviolence. He earned the nickname "Peace Ladd." In 1828 he became head of the American

Peace Society, an amalgamation of numerous smaller peace societies. In 1831 he wrote, "The cause of peace will obtain my zealous and unequivocal support."

But that same year Garrisonian nonviolence was put to another test by an uprising by an enslaved man in Virginia, Nat Turner, who killed at least fifty-four white men, women, and children in a four-day rebellion. Southerners blamed the Nat Turner incident on Lloyd Garrison. Garrison pointed out that slaves were motivated by the cruelty of slave owners and didn't need him to inspire an uprising. He said that the American people, by not stopping slavery, were to blame for the insurrection.

Garrison could not condone the use of violence and pointed out that Christ preached "returning good for evil." Also, such rebellions, as David Child argued, cost too many Black lives— 120 Black people were brutally slaughtered in revenge for the Turner uprising. Faced with the atrocity of slavery, it was difficult to condemn rebellion. The Black community was once again divided between Garrisonians and followers of David Walker. Garrison had the advantage that the Black community was largely religious and Garrison had the teachings of Jesus on his side. But Garrison also had Black support because he was sensitive to the idea that many people only objected to violence when it was carried out by Black people. Garrison argued that no one who praised the patriots of the American Revolution had the right to condemn slaves for fighting for their freedom. But this was a dubious argument among Garrisonians because most did not approve of the revolution.

Ladd, for example, did not hesitate to condemn the Revolutionary War. In an 1836 letter Garrison quoted Ladd to Isaac Knapp:

[Mr. Ladd] said he did not wish to take away any of the
laurels which adorned the brows of our revolutionary fathers;
but he was free to confess, that, while he deemed them to have
been most unfairly oppressed by the mother country, he could
not reconcile their warlike measures with the pacific principles
of the gospel of Christ.

In 1834, to Lloyd's satisfaction, the American Peace Society moved its headquarters to Boston, making the city the home of the peace movement in the US. Most of the Boston Clique worked closely with the Peace Society and spread the idea that Garrisonian abolition was an unflinching peace movement. In 1839 Lloyd claimed that "the Principles of non-resistance have taken root more deeply and spread more widely in Massachusetts than in any other state."

Garrison was right. In the 1830s, there were more and more prominent peace advocates in Massachusetts, not only in the Clique but others who agreed with them. Massachusetts had peace advocates before Garrison that were still being listened to. Noah Worcester, a Unitarian Minister who eventually settled in Brighton, across the Charles River from Cambridge, was of an earlier generation, a fifer at Bunker Hill, but grew up to be a prominent advocate for peace. His book, *A Solemn Review of the Customs of War*, published in 1814 and with numerous later editions, all under the pen name Philo Pacificus, was considered one of the most articulate arguments against war and was avidly read by Garrisonians. Worcester wrote:

For war is, in fact, a heathenish and savage custom, of the
most malignant, most desolating, and most horrible character.
It is the greatest curse, and results from the grossest delusions
that ever afflicted a guilty world.

Then there were peace advocates of the Garrison generation, such as Boston Unitarian minister Adin Ballou, a close associate of Garrison. He championed abolition through moral suasion and complete nonviolence. He was a prolific writer, and his work was read and admired throughout America and Europe. Russian novelist Leo Tolstoy, who devoted his later years to advocating for peace, was an admirer of both Garrison and Ballou. He had Ballou's work translated into Russian.

Like his friend Garrison, Ballou called for a return to the original teachings of Christianity, declaring, "We cannot employ carnal weapons nor any physical violence whatsoever not even for the preservation of our lives." Unlike Garrison, who was convinced that nonresistant ideas were gathering more and more followers, Ballou understood that his beliefs would never be popular. He began one of his books, *Christian Non-Resistance*, "Here is a little book in illustration and defense of a very unpopular doctrine."

Both Ballou and Garrison argued that if injury is done, it does not matter whether the recipient is innocent or guilty. "If it be in fact an injury, it is contrary to the doctrine of Christian non-resistance." Ballou argued that Jesus never contemplated passive resistance but "an active righteous moral resistance." Ballou believed in activism. This is the great misunderstanding about nonresistance. It is resisting through nonresistance, which some found to be a difficult concept. Pacifists such as Garrison and Ballou abhorred passivism.

Lloyd Garrison believed that a nonresistant had to be an abolitionist but an abolitionist did not have to be a nonresistant. If you opposed violence in all its forms, you opposed slavery. All the leading peace figures, such as Ladd and Ballou, were abolitionists. But many abolitionists, even in the Boston Clique, were not nonresistants. Maria Child, but not David, was passionately nonresistant. David, for the most part, was a good Garrisonian. But from time to time, when events seemed to call for it, he turned against nonresistance. This, no doubt, was distressing to Maria, who was a perfect nonresistant, at least in the early years, abhorring violence, the military, and politicians. But she only seldom complained to close friends about this difference. Garrison accepted this about Child. Not all his lieutenants could be expected to agree about everything.

Garrison had in common with Emerson and the transcendentalists the belief that everyone had to stand by their own conscience. Emerson did not give credit to Garrison for this very transcendental attitude. It might be true that Garrison was one-sided. But he accepted that everyone was not always on his side. When they weren't, he would devote great energy to trying to change their minds. He believed in the power of reason.

Many abolitionists started as nonresistants because that was part of the movement, but then they changed. It was a difficult code and some would accept the rejection of violence but not the rejection of politics. Or they would reject violence, but not in all cases. This flexibility allowed many more people to sign on to the movement. But it also might have created weak links that, at challenging moments, might cause the chain to disintegrate.

Samuel Gridley Howe, a doctor who founded the first school for the blind in the United States, was not a nonresistant, though he mixed with Garrisonians and especially transcendentalists. He made much of his exploits in the Greek Revolution and proudly displayed his battle sword in his living room. (Garrison had listed among the things a nonresistant should oppose, "all trophies won in battle.") Howe passionately believed in abolitionism but believed that force would have to be used. He even contemplated taking action himself.

The balding but youthful radical minister Theodore Parker, whose grandfather had commanded the militia against the British at Lexington (the grandfather's weapon was proudly displayed in his library), was a founding transcendentalist. In his Boston home he was building one of the best private libraries in the country. His door was open to men and women, Black or white, who wished to discuss any issue, and it was said that no matter what subject he was approached with, he showed a deep knowledge. He worked closely with Garrisonians on abolitionist causes and often stated that war was immoral. But he just as frequently spoke in favor of war if it was enlisted in the cause of freedom.

The Garrisonian movement accepted that it was going to take an assortment of militants with differing views to build an abolitionist movement. According to Maria Child, Maria Chapman used to say, "The Lord does his work by many instruments that I would not touch with a pair of tongs."

But it created a weak spot in their ranks. Later, when John Brown wanted to drive a wedge in the peace movement, he headed straight for Parker and Howe.

One of the problems some abolitionists had with nonresistance was that Lloyd Garrison's definition included rejecting all political activity. A nonresistant should not vote, hold office, or participate in government in any way. As Adin Ballou put it, a nonresistant "cannot be an officer, elector, agent, legal prose-cutor, passive constituent, or approver of any government, as a sworn or otherwise pledged supporter thereof, whose civil con-stitution and fundamental laws require, authorize, or tolerate war, slavery, capital punishment, or the infliction of any absolute personal injury."

This was not a new idea. The Shakers had, for a long time, re-fused to vote. The early Christians, a strictly nonviolent cult until Emperor Constantine converted the Roman Empire in the fourth century, considered it unchristian to participate in government in any way. While some abolitionists were searching for a political party and a candidate who would stand up to slaveholders, Lloyd Garrison usually refused to endorse any party or candidate.

Maria Child was a true Garrisonian, rejecting war, all forms of violence, and politics. Of course, the position of women was different because they could not vote, even if they wanted to. But Maria had always hated politics. In a short story, "Home and Politics," she wrote:

> It came in the form of political excitement; that pestilence, which is forever racing through our land, seeking whom it may devour; destroying happy homes, turning aside our intellectual strength from the calm and healthy pursuits of literature and science, blinding consciences, embittering hearts, rasping the tempers of men, and blighting half the talent of our country with its feverish breath.

Maria saw the connection between war and politics: "both arise from want of faith in spiritual weapons; both start with the idea that the outward can compel the inward; both seek to co-erce and restrain rather than to regenerate; hence in emergencies, their choice of weapons will be similar."

Some nonresistants refused jury duty because they did not want to participate in a violent and unjust system. The transcendentalists, led by Emerson and Thoreau, were also abolitionists who distrusted government and usually did not vote.

This boycott of politics and government posed a problem for many abolitionists such as Sumner, Higginson, and David Child. David did not agree with his wife or with Lloyd Garrison on this issue. He believed that voting, running for office, and political organizing were the means to effect a legal abolishment of slavery. Child had always been interested in politics and was an active member of the Whig Party.

Within the tight circle of the Boston Clique, there were many nonresistants and others who were sometimes nonresistants. Nonviolence was more popular than refusing to vote. Maria Chapman estimated that one percent of the Massachusetts Anti-Slavery Society refused to vote. Historians estimate that two hundred votes were withheld by nonresistants in Massachusetts elections, which usually would not have been enough to turn an election. The number of withheld votes would have been more than doubled if women had been allowed to vote.

But in the broader world of abolitionists, many rejected, partially or entirely, the Garrisonian creed of nonresistance. The Tappan brothers, Lewis and Arthur, wealthy businessmen who founded the American Anti-Slavery Society in New York, did not accept nonresistance, nor did most of the New York movement. To them, it was a Boston thing. Lewis Tappan, who also did not want to allow women to speak, feared Garrisonians would give all abolitionists a reputation as fanatics. He also thought nonresistants would have a destabilizing impact on society, which may have been Garrison's point.

Southerners feared abolitionists because, despite all evidence to the contrary, they were convinced that they were plotting violent Black insurrections. Even before he was known, southerners were convinced that all abolitionists were like John Brown.

Extravagant prices were offered for the capture of prominent abolitionists such as Lloyd Garrison. A $100,000 reward was offered for the capture of Arthur Tappan. He was not one of the more radical abolitionists, but the Tappan brothers were well known for an extensive campaign to deliver abolitionist literature by mail around the country. In the South, there were severe penalties for distributing *The Liberator* or other abolitionist literature. Mobs stormed post offices in search of abolitionist material. If they found any, it was burned in a large bonfire. Given the risks, Postmaster General Amos Kendall ruled that a post office could refuse delivery of abolitionist mail.

Simple book salesmen were attacked in the South and, in the tradition of the American Revolution, tarred and feathered on the suspicion of spreading abolitionist literature, even if none was found on them. Organized groups, an early precursor to the Ku Klux Klan, practiced violent intimidation of anyone who appeared to have abolitionist sympathies. Such groups, called Patrollers, starting in the Carolinas and Virginia in the eighteenth century, formed either from the poor white population or, as in Virginia, from cadets in the military academies. Originally the purpose of these vigilantes was to control the slave population, but in the 1830s they started to be used all over the South against abolitionists or suspected abolitionists.

The North was becoming just as violent as abolitionists took on issues of northern racism. In 1831 Arthur Tappan's summer home in New Haven, Connecticut, was attacked by a mob. In 1834 a mob broke into Lewis Tappan's home, removed his furniture, and burned it in the street.

By 1834 abolitionists in the North expected violence. Speakers, both men and women, frequently had eggs or even rocks thrown at them. Violent mobs would break up meetings. In 1835 Whittier was pelted with mud in Concord. It was becoming a way of life for abolitionists to bear attacks without in any way fighting back. The abolitionists were holding true to their beliefs.

These mobs were more spontaneous and less organized than the Patrollers in the South. But they were a challenge to nonresistants. They could not meet evil with evil but had to show Christ-like forgiveness or, at the very least, refuse to respond. This display of remarkable courage and principle earned them the admiration of some people in the North. It even caused some to join their ranks.

In 1835, just as the idea of nonviolence was spreading, there were so many attacks in the leading cities of the North that it was called "the mob year." That was the year it was announced that the British abolitionist George Thompson was going to speak in Boston. A delicate man with fine features and curly hair, Thompson was a devout nonresistant who had a reputation for lecturing the most militaristic crowds in England on peace principles. Lloyd Garrison had met him on a trip to England the previous summer and they became close friends. Lloyd had praised him lavishly on his return to Boston and anti-abolitionists feared Garrison's new discovery.

Garrison invited Thompson on a speaking tour of the US. Several venues refused to host him, but in August 1835, Thompson gave a speech in Julien Hall for the anniversary of the emancipation of the British West Indies. David Child was one of the speakers. Maria Child noticed suspiciously rough-looking men in the audience. When the event was over, the stairways were lined with men with cart whips and clubs.

A plan was hatched by the Boston Female Anti-Slavery Society to keep Thompson engaged in conversation with a crowd of women until he arrived at a place where he could slip behind a curtain that hid an exit. To cover his escape, the women, including Maria Child, remained there in conversation so that it would not be noticed that their British guest was gone. Maria Child recalled that "my heart, meanwhile, throbbed so violently, that I felt I should sink upon the floor." Meanwhile, Thompson was rushed away in a carriage.

The following October, a rumor of an address by Thompson at the Boston Female Anti-Slavery Society sent a mob to their office. The mob included numerous leading citizens from a Faneuil Hall meeting on how to stop Thompson from speaking. It was reported by the Boston press that the mob was comprised of "gentlemen of property and standing," from which the abolitionists derived the sarcastic term "respectable mobs."

The women continued with a scheduled meeting, and the "respectable mob" started throwing stones and other objects at them. Lloyd, with typical Garrisonian humor, told the mob that if any of them were women in disguise, he could get them seats at the meeting. Finally, the mayor of Boston, Theodore Lyman, always a friend of the moneyed class, arrived and told the women to go home, since he could not guarantee their safety. Maria

Chapman walked up to the mayor and said that a number of the mayor's personal friends seemed to be leading the mob. "Have you ever used your personal influence on them?" she asked him. The women dispersed, and, according to one account, when they were told that Thompson was no longer there, someone in the mob replied, "Well, Garrison is here." As they angrily shouted for him, he remained sitting calmly in his shop composing an editorial. Some abolitionists said they would renounce nonviolence and defend him. There were enough abolitionists to win a fight with the mob. But Garrison told them to remain calm and hold on to their belief in nonresistance.

Members of the mob dragged him through the streets with a rope, tearing his clothes, but he never raised a hand to defend himself, never showed fear or anger, stoically stumbling on until the police were finally able to get him away and secure him for the night in the jail.

Lloyd Garrison had shown Boston what it meant to be a nonresistant and, after that event, *The Liberator* saw an increase in subscribers and numerous more Bostonians joined his movement. Despite his stance against participating in politics and against his wishes, that fall, Lloyd Garrison became a write-in candidate for the state legislature. Maria Child wrote that mob violence had gained them supporters, or, as she put it, "conspired to do our work."

Wendell Phillips, the aristocrat with a mansion at the fashionable corner of Beacon Street and Walnut, watched the mob attack on Garrison. He was impressed with Garrison's steady comportment but appalled that the authorities did nothing to stop the mob. Two weeks later, he met Ann Terry Greene, a small but fierce member of the Boston Female Anti-Slavery

Society who had been at the meeting when they were attacked. Ann clarified abolitionist positions and explained what the meeting was about. Ann lived in the Chapmans' house and started inviting Phillips to their famous teas, where he met Lloyd Garrison. He and Garrison had frequent talks. Phillips abandoned Beacon Street parlors and became a regular at the Chapman teas. He conversed with other abolitionists and soon he was committed to the movement.

When new to the movement, Phillips used his law practice to defend abolitionists, but, in the nonresistant spirit, he eventually gave up his prestigious law practice because he felt it was an immoral involvement with government. How could it be wrong to serve on a jury and not be wrong to be a lawyer? No longer dazzling courtrooms, he became one of the movement's most eloquent speakers. His rhetoric was searing but his delivery calm and dignified. Softly, he called Daniel Webster, a Massachusetts congressman who vacillated on the slavery issue, "a great mass of dough." He called Dorchester-born congressman and later Massachusetts governor Edward Everett "a whining Spaniel." He became famous for these sharp and clever digs.

In 1837 Wendell and Ann married, partners in another abolitionist-style marriage at a time when there was much work to be done. Hostility to the movement had expanded their following and they needed to solidify this growth. Nonresistance was no longer just an abstract idea; it was an unusual and powerful method of conduct, and abolitionists were not just cranks; they were bold and courageous people.

In the mid-1830s they had more to worry about than just the violence in the North. In 1836 Americans in Texas broke away from Mexico and declared an independent nation. But for almost ten years, they struggled to join the United States and abolitionists struggled to stop them.

The Founding Fathers had intended for slavery to be contained in existing states and not spread to new territories. But as Maria Child had pointed out, the slave plantation was not based on sound agricultural practices and these plantations were constantly exhausting the soil. As long as there were seemingly limitless markets for sugar and cotton, slavers were in constant search of new land.

The principle of not expanding slavery was originally abandoned in 1820 with the Missouri Compromise. It happened again in 1837 when Arkansas was admitted as a slave state in exchange for Michigan statehood.

The fight between Texas and Mexico was presented by Texans and their southern supporters as a fight for freedom against the Mexican dictatorship. This was constantly asserted in the American press. In reality, the fight began in 1829 when the Mexican government abolished slavery. Many southern slaveholders had moved to Mexican-owned Texas, often with slaves. These American settlers were ready to fight, not to be free of dictatorial Mexico, but to be free from its antislavery law. Some of these settlers envisioned an independent nation, which was their stated goal, but many of the Texas rebels wanted Texas to be annexed to the United States as a slave state.

Annexing Texas as a slave state would upset the carefully constructed balance of slave and free states. This, of course, was only a balance in the Senate. Slave states still had more votes for the president in the Electoral College and more members in the House of Representatives because the Constitution of the United States provided that each slave be counted as three-fifths of a person. These added numbers were counted in the Electoral College and in the apportioning of House seats, even though the people they were based on could not vote.

Garrison called for a nationwide campaign by the Anti-Slavery Society to stop annexation. David Child and Benjamin Lundy led the campaign. David published a pamphlet with the testimony of Americans who had lived in Texas. In it, he asserted that the Mexicans didn't in any way mistreat them and that the only reason for the uprising was to establish slavery in Texas. In 1842 David Child wrote, "The statements made throughout the United States, of tyranny and oppression on the part of Mexico towards the American citizens in Texas, are slanderous falsehood."

David was a loyal Garrisonian in many ways, but he was never a nonresistant. Recalling his glory days fighting for Spain, he now contemplated fighting for Mexico. He wrote to the Mexican chargé d'affaires offering to raise either a Black regiment or an integrated one to fight for Mexico.

Benjamin Lundy thought he had a better idea.

In mid-April 1836 Lloyd Garrison attended a Clique tea at the Chapmans'. The Lorings were there, as were the Westons, Isaac Knapp, and numerous other abolitionists. The meeting lasted until eleven at night. Maria Child was there without David, and she announced that they were moving in a month with Benjamin Lundy to Matamoros, a fortified Mexican city near the Texas border at the mouth of the Rio Grande.

Lundy had envisioned a utopian community in the South —integrated—where free Blacks could earn a profit growing southern products. Sugar, cotton, and rice would be produced by industrious free men and would show southerners what the

South could be. In March 1835 Lundy had signed a contract with Mexico for 138,000 acres (more than 200 square miles) between the Rio Grande and Nueces Rivers, the Nueces Strip. He would be permitted to settle 250 families.

Garrison responded to Maria Child that night at the Chapmans', "What a hazardous project!" He had opposed this and similar projects by Lundy because they were a form of colonization, the situation was unstable, and a few hundred families would not be enough to alter people's attitudes. This opposition from Garrison made Lundy elated to enlist the Childs, loyal Garrisonian insiders. But weeks later, Texans defeated the Mexicans in the Battle of San Jacinto, gaining independence, and the Mexicans withdrew from Texas. For abolitionists, this fight was lost, and Lundy abandoned the Matamoros project. Though upset by the outcome in Texas, Maria Child was relieved not to be joining a commune.

At the same time, Lloyd Garrison had to contend with growing violence in the North, what he called "mobocracy." So far, the people in the movement had been exemplary in turning the other cheek. But this was more problematic than slave insurrections, which, despite the claims of slave owners, abolitionists had no part in. It was only a matter of time until an abolitionist would take arms against a mob and people would be killed. What would the abolitionist response be? In 1837 it happened.

Elijah Lovejoy was a Presbyterian minister who printed a newspaper in St. Louis, Missouri.

When he ran an editorial denouncing the lynching of a Black man named McIntosh, a mob destroyed the press in his print shop. Lovejoy moved across the Mississippi to Alton, Illinois. He started printing the antislavery *Alton Observer*. His was an unflinching, hard-punching kind of abolitionism that infuriated slavers and their supporters. He wrote:

> *as all men are born free, so all who are now held as slaves in this country, were BORN FREE, and that they are slaves now is the sin, not of those who introduced the race into this country, but of those, and those alone, who now hold them, and have held them in slavery from their birth.*

He drove off mobs with a rifle, but three times his press was thrown in the river. He wrote in a letter to *The Liberator* that it was with reluctance that he had decided that it was necessary to arm himself. This was disturbing news in Boston. Lovejoy was determined not to be driven away again. "I have concluded, after consultation with my friends, and earnestly seeking counsel of God to remain at Alton. . . . and if I die, I have determined to make my grave in Alton."

In November, his fourth printing press arrived by Mississippi riverboat. He stored it in a stone warehouse, and with the mayor's approval, he and twenty friends took turns guarding it with rifles day and night. One night, the mob attacked, gunfire was exchanged, and one of the mob was killed. Lovejoy came out of the warehouse to fire on an assailant who was setting fire to the roof. Several members of the mob fired at him first and killed him.

Abraham Lincoln in Springfield denounced "the mobocratic spirit" and called Lovejoy's murder "the most significant event that ever happened in the new world." Though this was clearly hyperbole, there was a widespread reaction, and this was a crisis for the nonviolent movement.

In Boston, James T. Austin, the one who tossed out Maria Child's book with tongs, called Lovejoy's murder a patriotic act. Others saluted Lovejoy as "a great martyr."

But Abby Kelley wrote a friend, "It was shocking to learn that Lovejoy defended himself—he had better to have died as did our savior." Lundy wrote, "While we are sensible that many others will disagree with us, we still feel ourselves bound to protest against the use of deadly weapons, for any purpose." Ladd denounced Lovejoy for the same reason.

Lloyd Garrison said that taking up arms, even in self-defense, was not a Christian act, and Lovejoy was therefore not a martyr. Lloyd wrote, "I am shocked and filled with sorrow to learn, that he first took life before he lost his own, and that this reliance for victory in the darkest hour of the conflict was upon powder and ball. Alas! Alas! If the Son of God could suffer himself to be led as a lamb to the slaughter, and to be nailed unresistingly to the accursed cross, surely we are bound to imitate his example even unto death, and by so doing we shall be eternally victorious."

Even abolitionists who were less committed to nonresistance could not support Lovejoy's actions. Lewis Tappan said Lovejoy "made a great mistake." Many abolitionist societies issued statements denouncing Lovejoy's use of deadly weapons.

Not all abolitionists agreed. Nonresistant Beriah Green gave a eulogy in which he called Lovejoy a Christian martyr. Waldo Emerson wrote in his journal of "The brave Lovejoy." He wrote that there were always men "ready enough to die for the silliest punctilio . . . but I sternly rejoice that one was bound to die for humanity and the rights of free speech and opinion."

It was a test, and for the most part, despite these few important dissenters, the Boston nonresistance abolitionists held to their principles. But how much longer would they be able to do this? They survived 1837, but surely there was more to come. As a result of the Lovejoy controversy, they decided that they needed to strengthen their nonresistance. Lloyd Garrison, Adin Ballou, William Ladd, and other notable pacifists formed the Nonresistance Society in Boston, which attacked abolitionists whenever they failed to uphold nonviolent principles. This was a central doctrine that needed to be defended.

Photo of David Lee Child, 1864.

Six

1838—

A SWEET SOLUTION

What effect would it have on the slave holders and their slaves, should the people of the United States of America and the inhabitants of Great Britain, refuse to purchase or make use of any goods that are the produce of Slavery?

—Elias Hicks, Long Island Quaker minister,
Observations on the Slavery of Africans and Their Descendents, 1811

If David Child's company had succeeded, 1838 might have been a landmark year in the history of abolition. That was David's plan. Poor David Child, imbued with earnest concern, energy, and passion for his ideals, hopped from one promising project to another and always failed—always found himself buried in a mountain of debt that consumed all of Maria's substantial earnings from writing. Never defeated, what was he going to try next?

Sugar beets.

Always adept at leaping from one frying pan to the next, David connected with George Kimball, a New Hampshire abolitionist, who had been planning to join him in Matamoros. Now Kimball had another idea for David Child. Affluent people in Alton, Illinois, the town where Lovejoy had made his stand, were interested in starting a sugar beet company. If Americans could be switched from cane sugar to beet sugar, this would be a blow to sugarcane slave plantations. The Alton group wanted to hire someone to go to Europe and learn everything about producing beet sugar. David Child, a fluent French speaker who had been raised on a farm, seemed ideal for the task.

In 1747 a Prussian chemist, Andreas Marggraf, found that certain beets contained sugar identical to that found in sugarcane. Europeans started producing beet sugar. The idea was embraced in France after they lost their leading sugarcane colony, Saint-Domingue (Haiti), and by 1830 beet sugar was nearly a craze in France. But the idea did not catch on in the US, where ample supplies of cane sugar were produced.

David resolved to establish a sugar beet industry in Massachusetts that could compete with southern sugarcane. If the industrial know-how of Massachusetts could produce the nation's granulated sugar and cotton textiles, why not beet sugar for the nation? This was not a purely political stance. It was an attempt by the always-indebted Child to at last put his finances on solid ground and run a profitable enterprise.

The boycotting and replacement of slave-produced commodities, if it had ever worked, might have ended slavery. Even before the Revolution, Quakers refused to use slave-grown products, especially cotton and cane sugar, but there were not enough Quakers for this to be an impactful boycott. But Quakers did not look for results. Unlike the abolitionists, Quakers were only concerned with doing what was morally right regardless of the consequences. In the early 1800s the boycott of cane sugar in Britain had an impact on the abolition of slavery, but West Indian sugar plantations were already struggling. In America, with the help of East Boston refineries, sugar was prospering. The boycott of cane would have to be widespread. At the 1833 National Anti-Slavery Convention in Philadelphia, the newly formed American Anti-Slavery Society issued its Declaration of Sentiments, which denounced all use of "carnal weapons" but also suggested ways to carry out the fight without violence. The Convention called for the boycotting of all slave products. For this to work, alternatives had to be produced on a large scale. A number of American abolitionists took an interest in beet sugar. A fair amount of molasses was also being produced from sorghum.

More than ten years before his Matamoros idea, Lundy persuaded free Black people to move to Haiti to develop a free-labor cotton industry. But like Thomas Paul, who had tried this before him, Lundy found that free Black people were Americans, had little in common with Haitians, and were not well-suited for Haiti. To Garrison and many of his supporters this was another unjust colonization scheme.

The Liberator advertised free-labor products and told readers where to buy them. In New England free-labor candy was made from maple sugar, and that has remained a popular tourist item to this day. Lucretia Mott always carried a small sachet of free-labor sugar in her purse to sweeten her tea.

The most promising abolitionist boycott was the effort to pressure the British to buy free-labor cotton from India. Britain was the leading consumer of slave-grown southern cotton. Though Indian cotton was of lower quality than American, it was making inroads in the market. Abolitionists were also persuading free Black people in the South to produce cotton. Free cotton was also being produced in Africa and the West Indies. If British and New England textile mills had been persuaded to boycott slave cotton, this might have ended slavery. But in reality, not enough free cotton could be produced to compete with southern slave production, and this was also the case with sugar and rice.

In 1837, the Illinois Beet Sugar Company was formed and sent David to Europe with a promise to cover all his expenses and pay him a comfortable salary. He seemed to be on his way to success and financial security. He spent almost two years learning in beet sugar factories in France, Belgium, and Germany. But Maria, back in America, faithfully waiting for his return, had little confidence in the project. She doubted that beet sugar would be profitable. In an 1837 letter to Louisa Loring, she wrote, "I have a sort of superstition that his customary bad luck will follow him in everything." Maria was also resentful. She longed to go to Europe. Her books were popular in England. But they could not afford for her to accompany him. Perhaps later, they thought. But always short of money, the opportunity never came. Maria Child never saw Europe.

While David Child was in Europe, the Illinois Beet Sugar Company vanished without Child receiving any money at all. In 1838, back in Boston, he formed a partnership with Boston investors Maximin Isnard, the French vice-consul in Boston, and Edward Church. Church had written a book in 1828, *Beet*

Sugar, promoting the industry and translating French works on the subject. Church had determined that Northampton, with the rich soil of the Connecticut River Valley, was the best spot in Massachusetts for their project.

In 1838, Child moved to Northampton, and the following year, just as she was enjoying friendships and activism in Boston, Maria reluctantly joined her husband in farming sugar beets. She had not been eager to move to Matamoros, but this might have been worse. The local people in Northampton were conservative and either disliked abolitionism or were indifferent to it. She missed the eccentric progressives of Boston.

At the end of the year she wrote to her brother, Convers, "If I were to choose my home, I certainly would not place it in the Valley of the Connecticut. It is true, the river is broad and clear, the hills majestic, and the whole aspect of outward nature most lovely. But oh! the narrowness, the bigotry of man!"

Unfortunately, David Child's investor became interested in something new that was happening in Northampton—growing mulberry trees for the cultivation of silk worms. In Massachusetts, which was known for its textiles, Northampton was to become a silk center. With little warning, though, the Northampton Silk Company went bankrupt. With them went Child's financial backing. At this point, David owed several hundred dollars for machinery from Europe that was sitting on a New York dock. Maria paid for it with the money she earned from *The Frugal Housewife*.

Despite the many setbacks, David forged ahead and formed the first American sugar beet company. They rented an acre of land and worked it dawn to dusk, but after backbreaking work they found that the soil was exhausted.

In this town Maria was still remembered as a famous author and treated with great deference. Then she began to circulate petitions against the annexation of Texas and for other abolitionist causes. The townsfolk responded swiftly with anger and coldness. They did not want an abolitionist in their midst.

Six months after moving there, she wrote a friend, "I have never been so discouraged about abolition, as since we came into this iron-bound Valley of the Connecticut. I have ceased to believe that public opinion will ever be sincerely reformed on the question till long after emancipation has taken place. I mean that for generations to come there will be a very large minority hostile to the claims of colored people."

Increasingly depressed, her dreams of a nonviolent revolution were beginning to fade. In October 1838 she wrote fellow non-resistant Angelina Grimké:

> *I do not believe the South will voluntarily relinquish her slaves, so long as the world stands. It [emancipation] must come through violence. I would it might be averted; but I am convinced it cannot be.*

On the other hand, only two months earlier she had written her close Boston friends, Francis and Sarah Shaw, who often discussed abolitionist theory with her, not to shun conversation with slaveholders but to seek it out and to engage in argument "with candor and courtesy." And the following year, while visiting Boston, she wrote to David, "We will strive with all our might, mind, and strength, to overthrow slavery; but we see, as clearly as the simplest problem in mathematics, that this object cannot be advanced by violating freedom of conscience" and went on to say of nonresistance, "It is strange to me that men do not perceive there is no alternative for free and honest minds."

Struggling just to meet their living expenses, Maria resolved to manufacture rock candy and peppermints from beet sugar, but it is not known if she managed to do this. They may not have had enough sugar. Their first season yielded only 1,300 pounds. In the winter of 1839–40, the crop was insufficient. Maria and David moved back to Boston and she looked for a teaching job. David returned to Northampton. Despite the anger and frustration about her marriage that she expressed to her friends, she was still writing David the kind of love letters she had written twenty years earlier when they began. She wrote him, "How lonesome I did feel. How I did long for you."

By spring 1840 they were both back in Northampton, better prepared for their second season. Their sugar had won an award of $100 (worth about $3,500 today) from the Massachusetts Agricultural Society, which also promised future financial support. More certain and more surprising was the support from Maria's father, who had always considered David a useless business disaster. Convers Sr., now in his mid-seventies, bought a farm with good land in Northampton for the three to live on and produce beet sugar. They now had two workers, two oxen and two horses, and a young Irish woman to help in the kitchen. But they could never produce enough sugar for the company to be profitable and they had to close in 1841.

Maria took a job in New York as the editor of the *National Anti-Slavery Standard*, the weekly newspaper of the National

Anti-Slavery Society. She lived with the family of Isaac T. Hopper, a Quaker leader of the Underground Railroad. In that house, she often met fugitive slaves on their way to somewhere else. She deeply enjoyed life in this abolitionist home and the contact with Black refugees, and she developed an infatuation with the Hoppers' barely adult son.

Maria was disillusioned with her husband. She wrote Francis Shaw, "For the last six or seven years my conviction has been constantly growing stronger that my husband's deficiencies in business matters are incurable." And to Louisa Loring she wrote, "Poor David! . . . He constantly reminds me of Emerson's remark that 'Some men expend infinite effort to arrive nowhere.'"

In 1843 David filed for bankruptcy. In June, all his possessions were sold at auction. Under the laws at the time, all of a wife's possessions belonged to the husband, so all of her possessions were sold as well—furniture, clothing, jewelry, even cherished mementos from fellow abolitionists. She now had almost nothing—almost. Because Convers Sr. had so little confidence in his son-in-law, before entering the partnership on Northampton sugar beets, he took the rights to her books.

Frederick Douglass, 1855.

Seven

1841—

BRINGING IT HOME

*It made me sad to find how the north aped
the customs of slavery.*

—Linda Brent, *Incidents in the Life
of a Slave Girl*, 1861

Unexpectedly, in 1841, the Boston abolition movement found a superstar. Frederick Bailey was born a slave in Maryland in 1818. He barely knew his mother, and his father, probably his mother's white owner, was unknown. He was a slave for twenty years. As a young man, when he first heard the word "abolitionist," he did not know what it meant. For some time, he wondered about the word. He later wrote in one of his memoirs, "It was always used in such connections as to make it an interesting word to me." He tried consulting a dictionary, which only told him that it was about "the act of abolishing." Abolishing what? He didn't know. He was afraid to ask anyone, because it was clear it was something he was not supposed to know about.

Although he was to become a Garrisonian nonresistant, as a sixteen-year-old slave, six feet one and powerfully built, he came to blows with one owner. He admitted to a sense of satisfaction from winning the fight. He wrote later, "I was nothing before. I am a man now." He called it "a glorious resurrection."

In 1838 he escaped to New York by train and steamboat. There, a free Black grocer and abolitionist, David Ruggles, hid him and found him work in New Bedford, Massachusetts, where he became Frederick Douglass. New Bedford had a sizable community of both escaped slaves and free Blacks. Skilled in the caulker trade, he could find work at the whaling port.

A few months after arriving in New Bedford, Frederick Douglass met an agent for *The Liberator*. He could not afford a subscription, but the agent gave it to him anyway. Douglass later said this paper changed his life and took a place for him next to the Bible. Garrison's clarity and power, his uncompromising stands, and the idea of moral suasion captivated the young refugee. Douglass had begun speaking to small groups of fellow slaves in Maryland. He had a natural affinity for both written and spoken words, and he was intrigued that this Lloyd Garrison was taking on slavery with the power of writing and speaking. Now he could expand and use his own skills.

In 1841 Garrison heard him speak in New Bedford and was so impressed that he invited him to speak at the Massachusetts Anti-Slavery Society's annual convention in Nantucket. Garrison was stunned by the talks he heard from Frederick Douglass at the two-day convention. "I shall never forget his first speech at the convention," Garrison later wrote. "The extraordinary emotion it excited in my own mind—the powerful impression it created upon a crowded auditory."

The two men had tremendous admiration for each other and they became the heart of the Garrisonian movement, speaking together and protesting together. Frederick and Lloyd went on speaking tours together, appearing every day. It became the leading abolitionist show, moving thousands of people. The lean, boney-faced Charles Remond had been the leading Black abolitionist speaker in Boston, often traveling with Garrison. But he could not compete with Douglass's physical presence, his musical baritone voice, the skill of his rhetoric, and the fact that he had been a slave and could tell firsthand what it was like. Douglass's eyes flashed with anger or melted with deep emotion. He stirred people.

Everyone wanted to hear Douglass. Going to a Douglass speech was an important cultural event. "I am a slave," he would say. "My back is scarred by the lash—that I could show you. I would I could make visible the wounds of the system upon my soul."

He also took on other Garrisonian causes—temperance and women's rights. "All great reforms go together," he would say.

In 1845 he published his first autobiography, *Narrative of the Life of Frederick Douglass, an American Slave*. It was an instant bestseller, reprinted nine times in its first three years. Slave narratives were a growing genre. At the time of the Douglass autobiography, an estimated sixty thousand slaves had escaped, and two hundred of them had written "slave narratives." One of the best-known ones was edited by Maria Child: *Incidents in the Life of a Slave Girl* by Linda Brent. But none had the sales of Douglass's.

Escaped slaves always had the looming threat of being kid-napped and returned to slavery. Lloyd Garrison and Wendell Phillips constantly worried about Douglass's safety. He had to write his autobiography in a way that would not put him at risk. He avoided details about where he was from and the identity of his owners. Because escaped slaves were often caught from letters or articles they had written, Wendell Phillips said he wanted to burn the manuscript before it was published.

In 1842 when Linda Brent escaped slavery to the North, she quickly felt "a chill to my enthusiasm about the free states." She pointed out that, at least in the South, when a Black person was made to ride a train in "a filthy box, behind white people" they didn't have to buy a ticket. It came as a hard blow to escaped slaves to discover that the whites in the North were also racists.

Abolitionists spoke openly about this. In 1833 both Maria Child, in her *Appeal*, and David Child, in his own essay on racism, angered Bostonians by decrying the racist treatment of free Blacks. This was a frequent subject for Garrison in *The Liberator*. In a typical Garrisonian quip, he wrote, "Hardly any doors but those of our State Prisons, were open to our colored brethren." And prophetically, in 1834 Garrison wrote that ab-olition would not be successful until "all unequal laws, having respect to the color of the skin, shall have been universally ex-punged from the Statute-books."

Even abolitionists frequently had racist attitudes. Thomas Higginson thought Blacks were intellectually inferior. Theodore Parker at times commented on the inferiority of Black people.

They were entitled to equal rights, but they were not equal, in their opinion.

Frederick Douglass sometimes detected racist attitudes among his fellow abolitionists:

> *When I first went among the abolitionists of New England, and began to travel, I found this prejudice very strong and very annoying. The abolitionists themselves were not entirely free from it, and I could see that they were nobly struggling against it. In their eagerness, sometimes, to show their contempt for the feeling, they proved that they had not entirely recovered from it. . . . When it was said to me, "Mr. Douglass, I will walk to meeting with you; I am not afraid of a black man," I could not help but thinking—seeing nothing very frightful in my appearance—"And why should you be?"*

But there were even clearer, more institutionalized forms of racism in New England to be challenged. In the first half of the nineteenth century, though about one in ten Bostonians was a free Black person, Blacks and whites did not mix. Maria Child never met a Black person until she became involved in abolitionism and met her first Black friends. Wendell Phillips never met any Black people, or for that matter, any poor people, until he started going door-to-door for the cause.

Lloyd Garrison was so unusual in his regular and close contact with Black people that it was sometimes thought he was Black. People would meet him and be surprised to see that he was white.

Increasingly, New England abolitionists were taking on the bigotry of New England. In the early 1840s, a lesser-known but equally forceful New Hampshire abolitionist, Stephen Foster, started working with Abby Kelley. They were well-suited team-mates, both from the uncompromising radical wing of the movement. They were both rousing speakers and worked easily together.

Stephen had abandoned the ministry to become an abolitionist. Although he personally believed in nonviolence, his speeches often led to violent riots. He was seriously beaten when attempting a speech in Portland, Maine, in 1842. A leading reason for popular anger at Foster was that, rather than speaking against the South, he focused on the complicity of New England churches. He would enter a church and denounce the minister and parishioners for failing to stand up to slavery. He frequently announced that the Methodist Episcopal Church, which did not stand up to slavery, was worse than any brothel in New York City. Foster once bragged that in a fifteen-month period he had twice been thrown out of second-story windows and four times jailed. He claimed that in that same period, he had been dragged out of churches twenty-four times. In all of this, he never once made any attempt to physically defend himself. Like Abby, he was a dedicated nonresistant.

An apparently perfect match, in 1845 they married, an abolitionist marriage of equal partners in an unyielding fight. They bought a farm in Worcester, Massachusetts, where they could raise their daughter. They shared in child-rearing, only occasionally leaving the girl with a relative, and campaigning together. More often, he stayed home and the more famous Abby went out on her own. They made their farm both a center for abolitionist meetings and a major station for the Underground Railroad to protect fugitive slaves.

Black movements against local racism, such as Nell's fight from the African Meeting House over segregated schools, could rely on Garrisonian support, help with petitions, and coverage in *The Liberator.* Nell was a soft-spoken, serious man. He was never a great speaker, which was an important attribute for abolitionists. But he was a good organizer and was known for his careful attention to details. He wrote the first books on Black history, such as *The Coloured Patriots of the American Revolution.*

Nell's great cause was the integration of Boston public schools. Starting in 1844 with the circulating of a citizen's petition, he fought for years, gathering support from both Black and white Bostonians. He also suffered the opposition of white and Black Bostonians. Some Blacks wanted their own separate schools. An angry white crowd assaulted one of Nell's meetings in the African Meeting House, where they regularly planned boycotts and petition drives.

Despite vehement opposition, the times seemed to be turning Nell's way. In 1843 Lowell High School, north of Boston, became the first integrated high school in America. But they had done that on their own. Nell wanted the courts to outlaw segregated schools, and he finally succeeded in 1855 when a bill passed in the Massachusetts legislature outlawing the practice of separate Black and white schools. Because of Nell, Boston became the first major city with integrated public schools. It was widely regarded as a triumph of good organization, though the issue was still fought over for the next hundred years.

Frederick Douglass, like other abolitionists, was dependent on the railroad for constant travel from one speaking engagement to the next. But here in abolitionist New England, he encountered what was called "the Jim Crow car."

The term Jim Crow is thought to have come from an 1828 minstrel song, "Jump Jim Crow," by a New Yorker, Thomas Dartmouth Rice, a popular white entertainer who performed minstrel shows in blackface. The term was first used for railroad cars for Black passengers in Massachusetts in 1841 and became a common term.

White abolitionists, especially Lloyd Garrison, and many Boston Black abolitionists, including Remond, Nell, and Douglass, became determined to integrate the railroad. Traveling with William Nell, Lloyd Garrison had moved to the Jim Crow car with him and afterward made a policy of always traveling in the Jim Crow car.

In 1841 Douglass and Garrisonian organizer John A. Collins bought train tickets from Newburyport to Dover, New Hampshire, for a speaking engagement at the county antislavery society. The two settled into a double seat until an angry conductor ordered Douglass to move to the Jim Crow car. Collins protested and the two refused to move. Five burly men were sent in to drag Douglass over Collins's body and, his clothes torn, threw him into the Jim Crow car. A kinder conductor went to the car to console Douglass, telling him that the practice wasn't that bad because, after all, many churches had "negro pews," another practice Boston Blacks had been protesting since Thomas Paul.

Weeks later, Douglass, with Collins and two other abolitionists, boarded a train at the Lynn depot. A conductor grabbed Douglass by the collar and ordered him to move. The perfect nonresistant in those days, Douglass used his powerful body to hold fast to the chair and said, "If you can give me any good reason why I should leave this car I will go willingly, but without such reason, I do not feel at liberty to leave, though you can do with me as you please, I shall not resist." Other passengers started repeating, "Give him the reason! Give him the reason!" The confused conductor uncertainly said, "because you are Black."

Six railroad men came and started beating Frederick, but he and Collins held so tight to their seat that the men ended up ripping it from the floor and throwing the two in their bench off the train to the ground.

The people of Lynn protested, and there were threats to boycott the railroad. Douglass and his wife, Anna, a free Black woman from Baltimore, and their small son and daughter, moved to Lynn. It was a fashionable Boston-area resort known for shoemaking. Some historians suggest that the move was because of the town's support for desegregating the trains, but abolitionist friends urged the move, thinking it was safer for a fugitive slave than Boston. Slave hunters focused on large ports where they could quickly ship a captive south.

Describing his experiences on Massachusetts trains became a standard part of Frederick's speech. Abolitionists began to ride every train in Massachusetts to test their policies. Stephen Foster launched a campaign to persuade white passengers to sit in Jim Crow cars. The abolitionists had learned a new technique. Quaker abolitionist James N. Buffum, who rode the trains, reported in the *National Anti-Slavery Standard* in New York, edited at the time by Maria Child, "I am convinced that the agitation growing out of these incidents will do much good. . . .

Everywhere I go, I hear men and women talking of these shameful transactions."

In addition to the rides, there were calls for boycotts. Maria Child wrote that white people should not ride any segregated transportation. Boycotts were particularly effective on this issue because alternative integrated transportation was easily available in Massachusetts. In 1842 *the Liberator* started publishing train schedules and noting which trains abused and segregated Black passengers. Soon all eight lines abandoned segregation.

The technique started to be used in churches that had backrow pews for Black worshippers. Abolitionists would go into these churches, whites taking Black pews and Blacks taking white ones. Frederick Douglass urged Black people to leave their Black churches and go to white ones and take white seats. If they were thrown out, that would create the kind of spectacle that turned public opinion. Sometimes Black worshippers would stand in the aisles, refusing to take Black seating. White members would sometimes walk out of segregated churches and create new integrated ones.

Even Blacks and whites walking together on the street was frowned on and denounced, and abolitionists responded by deliberately strolling together, which they called a "walk along." Henry Clarke Wright became an abolitionist in 1835 when he was denounced for having been seen on a Boston street walking with a Black woman.

Abolitionists also tried to break the taboo on Blacks and whites eating together by sitting together in Boston restaurants and boycotting ones that would not allow it.

Frederick Douglass believed they were making progress in the North. In 1849 in a Boston speech he said, "The time was, when I walked through the streets of Boston, I was liable to insult, if in company with a white person. To-day I have passed in company with my white friends, leaning on their arm and they on mine, and yet the first word from any quarter on account of the color of my skin I have not heard."

There were many fights to come, but it was clear that moral suasion had a better chance of working in Massachusetts than in the South.

Elizabeth Peabody.

Eight

1843—

KOOKY BOSTON

*You take it for granted that I am glad to be away from
the din and activity of Boston. But oh, how I have
hungered and thirsted after the good, warm abolitionist-
sympathy, which I found only there.*

—letter of Maria Child in Northampton
to Abby Kelley, October 1, 1838

In 1843 US President John Tyler, raised in a Virginia slave-holding family, came to town. Boston was not his town. At the moment, he was the most prominent slaveholder in America, and Boston abolitionists were there to confront him. But there were two Bostons, and the president was joined by notable Massachusetts figures who supported him. And there was a crowd cheering.

The occasion was the inauguration of a monument to the battle of Bunker Hill. Like the battle itself, the monument was not located on Bunker Hill but on neighboring Breed's Hill. It was the first monumental obelisk erected in the US.

The monument was not easily achieved. It was first proposed in 1823. Many people in Boston did not want such a monument to warfare to be built, and there was boisterous opposition to the project for years. William Ladd denounced the proposal as a monument "to barbarism and anti-Christian spirit." But in 1841 others would have to lead the protest because Ladd, while delivering a speech on peace in Portsmouth, New Hampshire, sank to his knees. He continued his speech until he fell over dead—he died speaking on nonviolence.

In 1843 a huge Boston ceremony marked the opening of the monument. A parade of sixty military companies with thirteen elderly survivors of the battle marched from downtown across the Charles River to Charlestown. Puffy Daniel Webster, "the mass of dough," otherwise known as the greatest lawyer in America, delivered a speech, which Lloyd Garrison walked out on, characterizing the event as "painful." He had written that he opposed "all monuments commemorative of victory over a fallen foe."

A swarm of abolitionists approached the president and demanded that he free his slaves. They had a petition that hundreds had signed demanding this "act of simple justice." They had other arguments against Tyler. He was a leading backer of Texas annexation. Blocking the annexation of Texas became the central goal of abolitionists. "People of the North! Will you permit it?" cried Benjamin Lundy. Massachusetts Representative and former president John Quincy Adams led the fight to block Texas. The Rhode Island and Vermont House delegations petitioned to stop annexation. Lloyd Garrison predicted that Texas would eventually be annexed and this would lead to "dissolution of the Union."

The southern press denounced Tyler's reception in Boston, with one Virginia paper calling it "a gross breach of hospitality." But they were not surprised in Virginia, where Bostonians were regarded as ill-mannered, politically and socially radical, and kooky in general. Tyler knew what he was in for when he decided to come to Boston. Among southern conservatives of the 1840s, Boston had a reputation similar to San Francisco in the 1960s. According to southerners, abolitionism was only one of the worst trends of godless northern fanaticism. Boston was a city of free love, immoral sexual relations, weird religious beliefs, bizarre and incomprehensible movements such as transcendentalism, women's rights, and other radical social beliefs, and weirdo communes where they tested their oddball dogmas.

Like all hyperbole, there was a little truth to all this. Most of the fringe ideas of the age—free love, socialism, utopian communities, a revised religion, spiritualism—all found their places in Boston. Boston radicals were seen as strange and colorful. Abigail Folsom was a notorious radical who showed up at Faneuil Hall and other venues to interrupt speakers and insist on women being heard. Emerson called her "the flea of conventions." She frequently punctuated her comments by shouting in a piercing screech, "It's the capitalists." Wendell Phillips often politely showed her to the door as she was shouting. She also shouted in churches, the state legislature, and other gatherings. She would go to prisons and shout in defense of inmates.

Her antics were widely reported as evidence that the abolitionists in Boston were crazy people. It was her screech that made her seem unbalanced, but in fact, Phillips, Douglass, and others respected her and what she had to say. In fact, the argument for slavery really was an argument of capitalism—the sanctity of property.

By 1840, spiritualism—the belief that insights into morals and religion could be gained by contacting the spirits of the dead—had settled into Boston. It was a new fad that would endure in America for most of the nineteenth century. Its followers were generally among the educated upper class. Lloyd Garrison and Maria Child were both spiritualists, though they never discussed it with each other until 1857. When Maria shyly broached the subject, Lloyd answered, "I shall say nothing to any one about your inquiries on the subject of Spiritual Manifestations. I am a firm believer in the reality of those Manifestations, after the many things I have witnessed, and the various tests I have seen applied." He even recommended his favorite medium, a woman in Hanover, Massachusetts, who came to Boston from time to time.

Garrison also corresponded with Susan B. Anthony on the subject. It was generally believed by spiritualists, and strongly believed by Garrison, that women were more spiritual than men. This was why mediums were always female. Susan Anthony was particularly interested in spiritualism because it was increasingly being embraced, especially in New England, as an underpinning of the women's movement. Spiritualism taught that women had a special force.

By 1843 Boston had grown to one hundred thousand people, it had a thriving port, and its wealthy class included the captains of American industry. It had a huge and profit-able trade with the port of New Orleans and brought in the slave-produced cotton that was the base of New England's dominating textile industry—massive mills that were devouring the rivers north of Boston. Sugar produced on southern slave plantations was crushed, boiled, put into blocks with New England-built machines, and shipped to the growing industrial port of East Boston where it was refined into granulated sugar. Sugar had been sold in cone-shaped blocks until the Boston refineries developed granulated sugar, which became in great demand. Molasses, the thick, dark syrup left after cooking off the crystals, was also shipped to Boston, where it was made into rum, the leading alcoholic drink in America. Boston rum, Boston granulated sugar, and New England textiles were important to the New England economy and a key to the success of Boston Harbor. None of this was a secret. Abolitionists; industrialists; dock, mill, and industry workers—all understood the importance of slavery to Boston's prosperity. To many Bostonians, abolitionists were radicals out to destroy the Boston and New England economy.

It was still a small city, less than a third the population of New York and smaller than Philadelphia or Baltimore. In nineteenth-century America, little Boston, along with far larger New York, was one of the country's great sources of wealth, providing the capital for development in the young nation, such as railroads. There was the Boston that cheered President Tyler and the one that denounced him. Abolitionists and anti-abolitionists lived side by side in most neighborhoods. Lloyd Garrison knew many of the people who were dragging him by rope. It may have been neighborhood people living east of the Common who smashed the window at Ticknor and Fields. Wendell Phillips was deeply disliked in his Beacon Hill neighborhood, where he was thought to be a class traitor and an enemy to his neighbors' prosperity.

Small though it was, Boston was also a center of American intellectual life and it had a remarkable number of intellectual hubs. The parlors of the aristocrats who discussed art and literature and thought they were the arbiters of culture were on one side of Beacon Hill and the African Meeting House was on the other side. The Chapmans and the Garrisons held tea downtown, and the ground floor of *The Liberator* became a bookstore where radicals met and could find the latest pamphlets and books on all the Garrisonian causes. Here, Black and white activists could meet and hear each other's ideas.

The wealthy who controlled the big libraries, being the leading old Boston families, were imbued with self-importance. As aristocrats, they were generally not open to rebellious new thinkers, and many important ideas went elsewhere. So did a few of their class, such as Wendell Phillips.

The transcendentalists were based farther out of town at Waldo Emerson's big white house in Concord. Though they also championed abolition and nonviolence, they were known as the true eccentrics. Emerson and Thoreau had been known as rare screwballs and pranksters since their student days at Harvard and never lost that image. Transcendentalism, chiefly defined by the writings of Emerson, was difficult to understand, and, to some, seemed esoteric. It was essentially a belief that intuition and spiritual thinking transcended empirical and material thinking. What you deduce from your inner feelings transcends what you observe or experience. As Emerson explained it, "What lies behind us, and what lies before us are tiny matters compared to what lies within us."

Though not always accessible, Emerson had a sharp wit that made him popular, as when he said, while trying to read Machiavelli, "The Florentine factions are as tiresome as the history of the Philadelphia fire-companies." Charles Dickens, in his *American Notes*, searching for a definition of transcendentalism, claimed that he had been told "whatever was unintelligible would certainly be transcendental." On the other hand, Emerson denounced the Dickens book for its "ignorance."

Maria Child, in an 1844 letter to a friend about the newest book by her old friend Waldo, wrote, "As usual, it is full of deep and original sayings, and touches of exceeding beauty. But, as usual, it takes away my strength, and makes me uncertain whether to hang myself or my gown over a chair." It was a marked contrast to Lloyd Garrison or Maria Child, whose writing was known for its clarity.

Yet, with the possible exception of Frederick Douglass, Emerson was the most popular speaker in America. The neoclassical portico at the entrance to his stately white house seemed appropriate. For it was the entrance to a temple not only of the great minds of Boston, but such people as Walt Whitman, Henry Wadsworth Longfellow, and Herman Melville also paid visits to talk with Emerson.

The Peabody sisters—Elizabeth, Mary, and Sophia—gathered their own circle of Boston intelligentsia. Their mother, a school teacher, had married young, and it was an unhappy marriage. She raised her three daughters to be independent. The girls grew up in Billerica, a town of twelve thousand a few miles inland from Boston, but connected by a newly built canal. In 1840 Elizabeth rented a brick townhouse at 13 West Street in

Boston. Though only a half block from the Common, this was known by the wealthy establishment as the wrong side of the Common. The townhouse was, in fact, across the street from a livery stable, but to Elizabeth this was the side to be on. It was around the corner from Washington Street, which was the heart of Boston publishing—really the heart of American publishing. On the corner, Elizabeth could say that she had a publishing office on Washington Street, and that gave her legitimacy in the publishing world.

To the frustration of some of the town's aristocracy, abolitionists did have wealthy backers, and with their help, the Peabodys created a bookstore on the ground floor, stocked not only with Boston books but also works from France, Germany, Italy, and Spain. This was one of the best bookstores in America. It was also a lending library. Upstairs, Mary ran a school, the most profitable venture in the house, and Sophia, a promising young artist, had a studio there too.

In the 1840s Wednesday nights were open house nights on West Street. The sisters drew leading figures, especially from the transcendentalist movement. They discussed plans, including establishing a new progressive church for Theodore Parker. Elizabeth became the publisher of Emerson's magazine, *The Dial*. Elizabeth was herself a transcendentalist. She wrote an article in *The Dial* in which she opined, "Why not begin to move the mountain of custom and convention?" She, like the other transcendentalists, questioned a wide variety of social and political conventions. She challenged moneyed Boston and asked, why not dare to be an abolitionist in Boston?

In addition to *The Dial*, she published an important abolitionist pamphlet, *Emancipation*, by William Ellery Channing. Channing was the leading Unitarian, a sect that challenged the established churches, even their belief in the deification of Christ.

The authors that Elizabeth Peabody published under her own imprint included Parker, Margaret Fuller, and Nathaniel Hawthorne, who had a greater interest in the Peabody sisters than in transcendentalism. According to legend, Hawthorne, who often railed against his Puritan ancestors, one day at West Street started to mutter about another outrage he had learned of in the archives of seventeenth-century New England—the early Puritans had forced women to wear a red letter A at least two inches in height if accused of adultery. Elizabeth, and possibly Maria Child, encouraged the handsome young author to write about this cruelty. Elizabeth became Hawthorne's first publisher. He worked with her on a collection of stories for children and two other books. *The Scarlet Letter*, the story of this outrage, started out as a short story and over time expanded to a novel.

The bookstore was a meeting place and mail drop for Boston's progressives; Parker and Emerson were regular visitors. The Peabody sisters were bringing the leading women writers in America to West Street. Sophia had been a child when, with her interest in art, she had gone to the studio of Francis Alexander and there met the famous writer, Maria Child, posing for a portrait. She was thrilled now to have Maria as a regular in the bookstore.

On Thursday mornings from 1839 until 1844, Margaret Fuller held an event she called "Conversations," in which women, young and old, famous and little known, were invited to discuss art, philosophy, religion, and even politics, which was revolutionary for a women's group. Among the participants, along with Maria Child, was Elizabeth Cady Stanton.

Stanton, from Johnstown, New York, was the daughter of Daniel Cady, a prominent lawyer. The Cady family moved to Albany, and then to Boston, and entertained abolitionists such as William Lloyd Garrison in their home. Elizabeth was informally educated in law by her father. In 1840 Lloyd Garrison described Elizabeth as "a fearless woman, and goes for woman's rights with all her soul."

One of the regulars at West Street was George Ripley. He had been the minister of a downtown Unitarian church on Purchase Street, near the Garrisons. In a city of celebrated ministers, he had garnered little reputation and considered himself a failure. He believed that the cause of his failure was that he was preaching in a "vicious society" in which ideas could not prosper. He proposed to build a different society, one that was free from "the extravagant worship of wealth." Ripley foresaw that the United States was heading toward a violent conflict. He did not foresee the fight so much over slavery as over wealth and poverty. The slavery issue, on one level, was also an economic conflict. To eliminate slavery, he believed, abolitionists first had to change the socioeconomic structure of the country. Ripley was a decade ahead of Karl Marx.

To many, he was an oddball. But he became a transcendentalist; transcendentalists were famous for their oddballs and, in the 1840s, with abolitionism expanding its base, the movement welcomed everyone.

Ripley was not without admirers, especially among the transcendentalists. Margaret Fuller, who had met him through Emerson in Concord, was a fan. When he started talking at West Street about his dream society, a utopian community, he drew other admirers. Abolitionists were out to change

American society and by the 1840s the idea of change was greatly broadening.

In 1841 Ripley began soliciting investors for a jointly owned dairy farm, Brook Farm, on 170 acres in West Roxbury. Those who went there described the space as verdant and beautiful. "The earth is a green garden, blossoming with many-colored delights," Hawthorne wrote. Ripley's idea was to have great intellectuals laboring with farmers while workers expanded their minds with books he would make available. Slave and free, Black and white, were only the beginning. This interracial society would destroy all class distinctions.

It was not a unique idea in 1841. There were a number of utopian communes being set up around the country, especially in New England, and most particularly in Boston. Most had both anti-racism and anti-classism as fundamental principles. Emerson, who never shied from sarcasm, said that there was "not a reading man but has a draft of a new community in his waistcoat pocket."

The Nonresistance Society alone generated five communities. One of the most successful and enduring was Adin Ballou's Hopedale, a socialist commune founded on the principles of peace and nonviolence. It finally went bankrupt in 1856, though the town of Hopedale, about twenty miles inland from Boston, still exists. It was an interracial society based on socialist concepts of shared labor and shared profit. Ballou said it was "a moral power antislavery society, radical and without compromise."

Hopedale residents owned their land, thirty buildings, and a schoolhouse. Like New England's giant textile mills, they built dams to generate power to operate their small shops, which produced shoes, boxes, and other simple items. As with the other utopian communities, they experimented with socialism. At first, they paid everyone the same. When this did not work well, they established different pay scales but with a maximum pay. Then a minimum income was established, with added income for work done.

Hawthorne, eager to leave his family, was one of the first to join Brook Farm. Hawthorne was not an abolitionist, though he was close to many who were. Hawthorne thought slavery was wrong and such a bad idea that it would one day fall under its own weight. This was a convenient belief, because it meant that he didn't have to do anything. He wrote in one of his diaries, "I am more an Abolitionist in feeling than in principle." He was not going to sacrifice his literary career for abolitionism like Maria Child. Finding the time and space to develop his writing was his singular ambition.

Donating $1,000, he moved to Brook Farm, hoping to have writing time while learning to milk cows and shovel manure. He discovered that he did not want to be a dairy farmer. He concluded, "Labor is the curse of this world, and nobody can muddle with it without becoming proportionately brutified." The lovely green summer over, in November he asked Ripley for a refund.

Fuller visited at least once a month but never joined the community, and Hawthorne found her lofty position irritating. Hawthorne regarded his time there as a wasted five months, but this was not exactly true. He came away with a book, *The Blithedale Romance*, a fictional satire of Brook Farm, in which a Margaret Fuller-like character is prominently featured. He described the people at the farm as "our little army of saints and martyrs." He also wrote, "Whatever might be our points of difference, we all of us seemed to have come to Blithedale with the one thrifty and laudable idea of wearing out our old clothes."

In his descriptions of the character generally thought to be Margaret Fuller, he was neither the first or last to betray a sexual attraction: "Her hair, which was dark, glossy, and of singular abundance," and the thrill of "one glimpse of a white shoulder." Some literary historians also suspect that Margaret was the basis for Hester Prynne, the beautiful, adulterous heroine of *The Scarlet Letter*. His physical description of her in the novel resembles his description of the earlier Margaret-like character.

But there was something else Hawthorne came away with. Sophia, the artistic youngest Peabody sister, under the spell of Margaret Fuller, had decided to move to Brook Farm, where she and Hawthorne spent time together. After Brook Farm, they met regularly at the Peabody parlor. This was awkward because it was widely known that Hawthorne's publisher, Elizabeth Peabody, was madly in love with him. And he had seemed to reciprocate before his summer in the commune, though he was, at the same time, courting another woman who was wealthy and beautiful.

After the commune, Nathaniel would check that the parlor on West Street was empty before he would go in with Sophia. Shy Sophia had landed a legendarily attractive and increasingly famous writer. They were married in the Peabody parlor, a tasteless or at least heartless choice, and Elizabeth did not attend. Off they went to Concord, where a house had been arranged for them by Waldo Emerson, and there they would dine on the fresh, luscious vegetables grown by Henry David Thoreau.

Boston love affairs at the time seemed fungible. Before Hawthorne, Elizabeth Peabody had been in love with an eloquent reformer named Horace Mann, who had not entirely recovered from the death of his first wife. Once Horace became closely involved with Elizabeth, he took up the cause of education for which he became famous. Then he left her and married her sister Mary, the teacher. Elizabeth was the brilliant Peabody who never married. Mann fought for a public school system with racial and economic integration. He made the Massachusetts public school system the model for the country. He was also an abolitionist, but not of the Garrisonian kind. He was active in the Whig party and served in the Massachusetts legislature.

Elizabeth and Nathaniel would have been one of those contemporary marriages of the Boston intelligentsia—two strong people with their own projects sharing ideas and ideals. Sophia, whom he condescendingly referred to as his "little dove," tended to idolize people. She idolized Margaret Fuller, which irritated Hawthorne but she also idolized him and spent her life trying to please her husband.

Elizabeth Peabody had brought the writings of her young protégé, Hawthorne, to Emerson. The two started taking long strolls together for the purpose of arguing. They had much in common. As writers they both believed in the new school of Romanticism, which praised the individual and the importance of nature. A fundamental disagreement was that Emerson believed that human beings were essentially good and had to find their goodness, and Hawthorne thought that evil lurked within every individual. They could debate these things. In 1842 the cryptic guru of Concord pronounced, "Nathaniel Hawthorne's reputation as a writer is a very pleasing fact, because his writing is not good for anything, and this is a tribute to the man."

Emerson lived in a world of activism. Amid transcendentalism, the Boston Clique, the African Meeting House, and feminists at the bookstore, Hawthorne and Sophia were rubbing elbows with all of these people and yet involved with none of it. Hawthorne would fish in a rowboat on the Concord River with abolitionists such as William Ellery Channing and later wrote, "Strange and happy times were those."

While Hawthorne was sidestepping the issues, transcendentalists were taking on a huge basket of thorny subjects. With the help of Elizabeth Peabody, Bronson Alcott, one of the early transcendentalists, established the Temple School. This school rejected lecturing and taught through conversation. In one famous incident, Alcott tried to teach that it was harder to cause pain than to receive it, and he demonstrated this by having an errant schoolboy rap his own knuckles with a ruler. The school was subjected to severe criticism and eventually almost all the parents withdrew their students. This was a blow to Elizabeth Peabody's hope for a transcendentalist education system. But Alcott pushed on.

A dedicated transcendentalist and abolitionist and a crusader for a vegetarian diet, Alcott moved to Concord, wrote lengthy tracts on transcendentalism, and, in 1843, started his own utopian community, Fruitlands, where people only wore linen to avoid supporting slavery. The farm was not only vegetarian; its residents refused to use animals for farm work on the grounds that it was cruel to animals and farmed by hand. Cows were not to be milked, nor were fields to be fertilized with manure. Bees were not to be robbed of their honey, nor could their combs be taken, so there was no wax for candles. This was not a problem because Fruitlands rejected artificial lighting, believing that God intended certain hours to be dark.

Initially, Alcott had wanted his community to be completely open sexually, not concerned with such things as the bonds of marriage.

A Vermonter, John Humphrey Noyes, established a community in Oneida, New York, for what he called "complex marriage," group sex. But it didn't catch on in Boston. Brook Farm had also toyed with this idea but turned against it. It was rejected by Fruitlands residents, including Bronson's wife. Since there was to be no free love, Bronson decided there should be no love at all, and the Fruitlands community was to be celibate. The ninety-acre farm in Harvard, Massachusetts, about twenty-five miles northwest of Boston, lasted only seven months. Years later Higginson wrote, "During many years the public was scarcely in the habit of taking Mr. Alcott seriously." Yet Alcott and Emerson remained close.

Despite all this intellectual ferment, life in Concord, which Alcott liked to call Concordia and Hawthorne said was Eden, resembled a French comedy. In 1841 twenty-four-year-old Henry Thoreau, after he moved into the Emerson house as a handyman, started flirting, and seemed to even be in love, with Waldo's wife, Lidian. After two years, growing tired of having Henry in his house flirting with his wife, Waldo arranged for Thoreau to become a tutor for a family he knew on Staten Island. While away, Thoreau wrote a love letter to Lidian, who crushed him with a letter explaining that she did not share his feelings.

Margaret Fuller moved into Emerson's house and began taking long, romantic walks with him. But Emerson's love did not seem reciprocated. He wrote in his journal:

> *These strange, cold-warm, attractive-repelling conversations with Margaret, whom I always admire, most revere when I nearest see, and sometimes love,—yet whom I freeze, and who freezes me to silence when we seem to promise to come nearest.*

Later, she ventured across to the Hawthorne house, a pig farm that Bronson Alcott had sold him, where she and Nathaniel flirted, while Sophia remained in awe of Margaret, and Emerson became jealous of Nathaniel.

Henry Thoreau was a nineteenth-century hippie with wild hair and scruffy clothing. He often advised youth not to listen to older people because they had nothing to offer, though he often deliberately copied the older Alcott or Emerson. Friends often ridiculed his beaklike nose. In his 1842 journal, Hawthorne described Thoreau as "long-nosed, queer mouthed, and with uncouth and somewhat rustic, although courteous manners." But he also added that his homeliness was "of an honest and agreeable fashion, and becomes him much better than beauty."

Thoreau had a certain hipness to his mastery of current issues. A brilliant mind is seductive. Alcott's young, aspiring writer daughter, Louisa May, was in love with Thoreau. She also, for a time, fell under the spell of Emerson. When Thoreau wanted to seduce a woman, he would take her on his pond in the boat he and his brother had built, the two-masted *Muskataquid*. He would place Louisa on the bow and explain the natural sights as they drifted. Sometimes, he would serenade her with his flute. Sometimes, he would stop to fish. Thoreau had an instinct for finding and luring fish.

Like everyone else he pursued Margaret Fuller even while he was chasing Lidian and Louisa was chasing him. Fuller recalled pleasant evenings paddling around the pond.

Thoreau and his brother took the *Muskataquid* down the Concord to the Merrimack and made their way on the Merrimack into New Hampshire. From that trip he wrote *A Week on the Concord and Merrimack Rivers,* one of the earliest and greatest environmental books, about a river destroyed by dams and textile mills.

Then he sold the *Muskataquid* to Hawthorne so he could give boat rides to Margaret Fuller. The problem with Fuller, who always looked radiant in the latest Boston fashion, was that she did not believe in marriage and had no desire to be in a couple. This was at a time when other single women were considered pitiable. She was brilliant but never easy, as Emerson often pointed out. Famously she once said, "I now know all the people worth knowing in America, and I find no intellect comparable to my own."

Then the unexpected happened. She fell in love with a younger man, twenty-two-year-old Samuel Ward, and then, more unexpectedly, he fell out of love with her, a crushing disappointment.

For all the social experiments and new ideas, the idea that was most firmly taking hold was nonviolent abolitionism. In the 1840s it was a central creed at Brook Farm, Hopedale, Fruitland, and all the other communes.

Even Emerson, who, unlike Thoreau, had been more about philosophical musing than political activism, was changing. Despite strong feelings against slavery, Emerson had not been a dedicated abolitionist. Now that changed. In his August 1844 speech at the Concord courthouse celebrating British emancipation, he invoked reason to the cause with his customary acidic eloquence. It is considered his beginning as an abolitionist. His speech began, "We are met to exchange congratulations on the anniversary of an event singular in the history of civilization; a day of reason; of the clear light; of that which makes us better than a flock of birds and beasts."

He became increasingly outspoken on the subject, drawing into a close collaboration with the Boston Clique. He also became a strong supporter of Frederick Douglass. As one of the most popular speakers in America, Emerson was becoming an important ally. All these different Boston groups were becoming one voice for nonviolent abolitionism.

An 1870 photograph of an 1846 daguerreotype of Margaret Fuller by John Plumbe, Jr., shortly before sailing to Europe.

Nine

1845—

MARGARET'S GOOD YEAR

I felt a delightful glow as if I had put a good deal of my
true life in it, as if, suppose I went away now, the
measure of my foot-print would be left on the earth.
—Margaret Fuller, 1844, on the completion of
Woman in the Nineteenth Century

Bad years are often good years for journalists. The year 1845 was a bad one for abolitionists because Texas was annexed after a ten-year fight, and a bad year for non-resistants because the US was amassing an army to attack Mexico and steal more of its land. But it was a good year for Margaret Fuller, who, with Horace Greeley's *New-York Daily Tribune*, took on racism, women's rights, and issues of poverty, and had a landmark book published that is still studied today. She became the first woman to be a star journalist.

After David Child's calamitous bankruptcy in 1843, Maria realized that she needed to separate her finances from her disastrous husband, and though she did not want to divorce him, she was able to get a financial separation. This was not an easy thing for a woman to accomplish in the nineteenth century, but once she did, she was not really broke, because her father had managed to get control of her book royalties. For the first time since their marriage, she could spend her earnings rather than turn them over to David's debts.

As editor, she made the *National Anti-Slavery Standard* a forum for both Black and white abolitionists. Frederick Douglass and William Nell were prominently featured. The most popular section in the *Standard* was a column she wrote called "Letters from New York," a feature that has been imitated by magazines ever since. These sketches took on her many causes. They were about Black people, but also women's rights, the mistreatment of Native Americans, Irish immigrants, and Jews. She also wrote about cruelty to dogs. And, at times, she wrote simply about scenes in New York.

Under Maria's direction the readership of the *Standard* grew to a circulation of 6,000—about twice that of *The Liberator*. But she was worn out by internecine squabbles between Boston and New York, even with her Boston friends, on nonviolence, nonvoting, women's rights, and a dozen other issues she needed to juggle as editor of one of the leading abolitionist publications. In 1842 Maria Child wrote Maria Chapman that she did not care if the various factions of the Clique criticized her: "I thank God more and more, that he gives me the power and the will to be an individual." But in 1843 Maria decided that her energy was being dissipated by squabbles and she resigned from the *Standard* and resolved to concentrate on her literary career.

Now, while the abolitionists were in their great campaign against Texas annexation, she just wanted to be a writer—like Nathaniel Hawthorne.

David Child took over as editor of the *Standard*. Abby Kelley objected to the appointment of David, saying that he had "a killing influence on everything he touches."

Once editor, David infuriated Kelly and other Garrisonians with editorials advocating what he called the "stay inner" position, stating that abolitionists should become members of churches and political parties and try to change them from within. This stance was the opposite of the nonresistant position. Opposition to his stay inner position and especially to his participation in the Whig Party became so vehement that he was forced to resign.

In 1844 Margaret Fuller moved to New York to write for Horace Greeley's *New-York Daily Tribune* and she and Maria Child renewed their Boston friendship. Fuller lived with Greeley and his wife in a quaint cottage on a wooded spot by the East River. "How anything so old and picturesque has been allowed to remain standing near New York so long, I cannot imagine," wrote Maria Child in a letter.

Despite Maria Child's supposed retirement from fighting for causes, she and Margaret Fuller became close friends, bonding over social issues such as poverty and racism in New York and the plight of young women who had come to New York looking for employment and ended up as prostitutes. In 1845 Fuller published *Women in the Nineteenth Century*, which endures as one of the great feminist essays. Fuller said she was greatly influenced by Maria Child's two-volume 1835 *History of the Condition of Women* that she had read at the Peabody bookstore.

————

Maria Child was enjoying her literary life but abolitionists knew that the slavers would not stop with Texas and they would have to mobilize for a larger fight, one Child would not be able to stay out of.

There was no hotter issue in the 1840s than the annexation of Texas. While pro-slave forces were plotting to expand slavery, Garrison began talking of "disunion." "Free states," he argued, "could not in good conscience participate in a union with slavers." In January 1845, at an anti-Texas rally at Faneuil Hall, Lloyd Garrison found himself supported by a larger crowd than he had ever experienced before. People were angry about this issue, this plot to steal land from Mexico in order to spread slavery. On the other hand, Senator John C. Calhoun, one of the Washington architects of annexation, started saying that if the North interfered with southern aspirations, the South should secede. Battle lines were being drawn.

Waldo Emerson, the new Waldo Emerson, even visited Lloyd Garrison in his "dingy" office, as Emerson put it, and discussed strategy. Emerson had respect for Garrison but had thought he was a bit too much—too intense, too demanding. Now with slavers grabbing Texas and out for more, Emerson was understanding Garrison. They had to work together.

The Texas issue was driving many northerners to abolitionism. In Boston activists were pushing their families to do more. Ann urged Wendell Phillips to give more speeches, knock on more doors, and raise more money. Maria Child introduced her niece, Mary Elizabeth Preston, whom she had tutored in abolitionism since childhood in Maine, to George Luther Stearns, the richest man in their hometown, Medford. In 1843 they

married, and Mary turned her wealthy husband into a confirmed abolitionist too. In 1844, the poet James Russell Lowell
married Maria White, who was not only an aspiring poet but a
dedicated abolitionist, and she brought her gifted husband, one
of the leading poets in America, to the cause.

In 1845, when Texas became the twenty-eighth state, it
became clear that the plans of the Boston Clique had gone wrong.
Instead of convincing the nation of their argument, they were
only convincing northerners, while southerners were becoming
increasingly aggressive. America was becoming two camps firmly
opposed to each other.

Abolitionists had never fought harder in Boston, throughout
the North, and in Washington led by John Quincy Adams. But
they had lost. It took almost ten years, but in the end, the slavers had too much political might. Garrison predicted that the
move would ultimately lead to a civil war. In *The Liberator*, he
described the annexation as "a crime unsurpassed in the annals
of human depravity." He called for the people of Massachusetts to withdraw their senators and congressmen "and treat the
government as a nullity." He declared, "NO UNION WITH
SLAVE-HOLDERS."

But the slavers were soon to surpass this crime with an even
bigger one.

Henry David Thoreau.

Ten

1848—

A ROPE OF SAND

Let your life be friction to stop the machine.
—Henry David Thoreau, *Civil Disobedience*, 1849

J ust as the abolitionists had always predicted, the annexation of Texas led to a larger war with Mexico that lasted until 1848. The Mexicans did not go to war to take back Texas but to defend themselves from the American ambition to take even more.

It was a time of great mobilization for Boston's abolitionists. At a January 1845 anti-Texas rally at Faneuil Hall, Charles Sumner, in a thunderous speech, launched his political career. He was a large man, known for his athleticism, and was said to have swum the Niagara River just before the Falls. Higginson described him as having "a grand, imposing presence, strong health, and athletic habits." Some said he was humorless; others said he was earnest, but he had a florid speaking style that raised emotions on both sides.

Sumner had been seen as an aristocrat. Boston-born from a family that descended from Puritans, grandson of a Revolutionary War combatant, a Harvard graduate of no distinction, it was Texas that threw him into the forefront. Like David Child, he had been active in the Whig Party. He was also active in the peace movement, but it was thought, contrary to the counseling of Garrison, that he could juggle nonresistance and politics. John Quincy Adams took him under his wing and brought him to the antislavery cause. From that day in Faneuil Hall over the Texas issue, he became a notable voice for abolitionism.

In 1846 President Polk invaded Mexico and then asked Congress for a declaration of war. The Democratic Party and its slave interest supported war. The only votes in Congress against a declaration of war came from fourteen Whigs led by John Quincy Adams. Despite the many whose consciences troubled them, there was considerable enthusiasm for war, even in northern states. Ohio and Illinois quickly raised large numbers of volunteers.

The war that the US called the Mexican War and the Mexicans called the North American Intervention left an indelible stain on both countries. There was no way to escape the clear fact that a powerful country was bullying a weaker one. Mexico lost about half of its territory—albeit the underpopulated half. According to Mexican history, it was stolen. According to US history, it was purchased. They were both right.

Mexico was forced into a war it could not afford. Partly because it had lost its tobacco monopoly, the government was bankrupt and in a state of economic upheaval that led to constant overthrows of the government, including during the war. The Mexicans armed themselves with old-fashioned firearms from the Napoleonic Wars that the French sold them at a low price. For cavalry engagements, they rented horses. They could not afford to maintain herds. General Santa Anna, who wore resplendent, ornamented uniforms, sometimes paid his soldiers with his personal money and gave them impressive uniforms as well. They looked dazzling in an attack with their old weapons. The American soldiers were impressed when they caught sight of the Mexican Army and then shocked when they saw with what they were fighting.

The two leading newspapers in New York, the *New-York Evening Post* and the *New-York Daily Tribune*, opposed the war. In Boston, aside from John Quincy Adams, who was almost eighty years old, Garrison was the most searing voice against the war. He even compromised his principles of nonresistance, to an extent, by cheering on the Mexicans. James Russell Lowell took to writing satirical poems in a folksy voice, denouncing the war and calling for disunion:

> *Ef I'd my way I had ruther,*
> *We should go to work an' part—*
> *They take one way we take 'tother*
> *Guess it wouldn't break my heart!*

The leaders of the Boston Clique—Garrison, Wendell Phillips, Charles Remond, and Frederick Douglass—spoke out regularly and powerfully against the war. Frederick Douglass called it "disgracefull" and said that Congress should be petitioned to recall troops from Mexico immediately.

A splinter group from the newly formed Liberty Party, the Liberty League, called for the disbanding of the armed forces.

Many abolitionists declared themselves opposed to the use of armed forces. Gerrit Smith, a wealthy New York state abolitionist who considered himself a nonresistant but did not renounce involvement in political parties, was elected President of the Liberty League. Theodore Parker, who usually rejected nonresistance, now declared, like a nonresistant, that all war was wrong. Charles Sumner launched a newspaper campaign against the war that he called "a wicked act." And when the party nominated Zachary Taylor, who had been a general in the Mexican War, for president, in 1848, Sumner withdrew from the Whigs. Many Whigs, including Illinois congressman Abraham Lincoln, opposed the war. Garrison called for dissolving the Union and creating a new country of free states only. Many accused him of treason.

Garrison claimed that it was an unpopular war. In reality, though it was hated by some, it was cheered by others. Both Zachary Taylor and Franklin Pierce based their successful campaigns for president on having been officers in the Mexican War. Both undistinguished presidencies lent credence to Garrison's early argument in reference to Jackson that a military career did not qualify a candidate for president. General Winfield Scott, who lost to Pierce, was also famous for commanding the army in the Mexican War.

Other officers who served in the Mexican War felt less proud of it. Ulysses S. Grant, who served in the war along with Robert E. Lee, thought the war was a disgrace. Years later, he wrote in his memoirs that the Civil War was "largely the outgrowth of the Mexican War." He wrote, "Nations, like individuals, are punished for their transgressions."

At the time of the war, abolitionists, including Charles Sumner in Boston and John Quincy Adams in the House,

denounced it. In February 1848, Adams died, but the seat was
not lost. He was replaced by Horace Mann. Of course, Mann
did not have the prestige of an ex-president who was the son
of a Founding Father, but he was a solid voice for abolition.
On taking office, he said, "I think the country is to experience
serious times. Interference with slavery will excite civil commo-
tion in the South. But it is best to interfere. Now is the time to
see whether the Union is a rope of sand or a band of steel."

Abolitionists looked for ways to resist the government. Refusal to pay taxes was not a new idea in America. It was much
discussed before the American Revolution. Free Black people
frequently considered it to protest segregated schools and transportation. But the idea arose with new energy during the Mexican War. In Concord, Emerson did not believe in refusing to
pay taxes. Frederick Douglass denounced people for protesting
the war and paying taxes anyway. Bronson Alcott refused to pay
taxes, and then Thoreau decided to do the same. Alcott's original stance did not get much attention because a neighbor paid
his debt and he did not go to jail. Henry Thoreau, however, had
one of the most famous one-night jail stays in American history.
He chatted through the night with the other inmates and the
next morning, his aunt paid the tax and he left. It did not launch
a widespread tax rebellion, not even among transcendentalists.
But it did give Thoreau a lasting reputation as a rebel and war
resister, even in modern times, though he did not always live up
to that image.

The experience led Thoreau to write a book, published by
Elizabeth Peabody in 1849, called *Resistance to Civil Government*. It later became famous as *Civil Disobedience*. The book
argues that an individual should not allow government to coerce

people into acquiescing to measures that they know are wrong. Thoreau used the Mexican War as an example. When government is wrong, it must be resisted. He lays out the groundwork for nonviolent resistance—when government is wrong, it can be stopped if people refuse to cooperate. The Mexican War, one of the most unjustifiable wars in history, produced one of the most influential books, a bible to nonviolent resistance with its message, "A minority is powerless while it conforms to the majority; but it is irresistible when it clogs by its whole weight." Going to jail was a way of resisting. He wrote, "Under a government that imprisons any unjustly, the true place for a just man is also a prison." The small book was studied by Tolstoy, and then by Mohandas Gandhi and Martin Luther King Jr., both of whom went to jail.

Opponents of the war knew that Mexico could not win. The only possibility was to stop the war. The Mexicans knew that too. Even during the war, the bankrupt Mexican government was continually changing hands. Soldiers were underfed. There were numerous regional rebellions against the government. The political establishment, fearing resistance would break down to local guerrilla armies, which would cause chaos for years, negotiated a peace. The war ended with the 1848 Treaty of Guadalupe Hidalgo. At the surrender, Pedro María de Anaya, a Mexican official, said to the Americans, "If I still had ammunition, you would not be here."

The US agreed to pay $15 million (worth about $600 million today) directly to the Mexican government, plus $3.5 million in debts the Mexican government owed Americans. This was enough to stabilize the Mexican economy and the Mexican government. But half of Mexico was now in American hands and the Americans hoped to turn it into a huge slave area, which they could control by revitalizing the genocidal practices of Andrew Jackson against the native population. To people such as David Child, Emerson, and Garrison, who had long asserted that America was failing to live up to its promise of liberty, this was a most vile example.

The future of America was on the line. The slave side saw an opportunity to build a continental slave nation. Abolitionists saw this as the last chance to save America. This is why Grant saw this as the beginning of the Civil War. Frederick Douglass agreed and wrote in 1848, "Sure as there is a God of justice, we shall not go unpunished; the penalty is certain; we cannot escape; a terrible retribution awaits us."

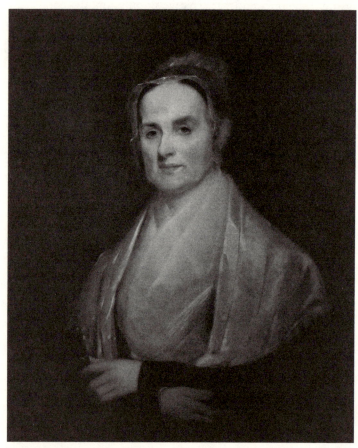

Lucretia Coffin Mott. 1842, oil on canvas, by Joseph Kyle.

Eleven

1848—

TIME FOR CHANGE

The slumber is broken and the sleeper has risen
The day of the Goth and the Vandal is o'er
And old earth feels the tread of freedom once more
—Elizabeth Cady Stanton, Seneca Falls, 1848

In a speech in Rochester, New York, in 1848, Frederick Douglass, who had recently been to Europe, said, "We live in stirring times, and amid thrilling events."

It was a time of upheaval and reform. In 1848 violent pro-democracy revolutions challenged old oligarchies throughout Europe. It was called "the Springtime of Nations." This was also the year that Karl Marx and Friedrich Engels published *The Communist Manifesto*—"Working men of all countries unite!"

In America, engulfed in an epic battle over the new territories, one of the most articulate voices for abolition, feminism, and other progressive causes was lost in 1846 when Horace Greeley sent Margaret Fuller to Rome for the *New-York Daily Tribune*. She was the first full-time foreign correspondent to work for an American newspaper. Rome, like much of Europe, was in the midst of a revolution, establishing a republic to replace the Papal dictatorship. She filed more than thirty dispatches—stories on the Roman Revolution and other events and interesting people in Europe, such as Elizabeth Barrett and Robert Browning and author George Sand, pen name for Amantine Lucile Aurore Dupin de Francueil, the French woman writer who took a male pen name. Sand's lack of feminist fervor disappointed Margaret. Miraculously, Fuller fell in love and married a Roman, the Marchese Giovanni Ossoli, and they had a son, Angelino.

From 1848 to the early 1850s, large and weighty conventions were called to change the world. "Peace conferences" against war and promoting nonviolence were held in London, Brussels, Frankfurt, and Paris, featuring prominent figures, such as author Victor Hugo in Paris, who was also an abolitionist. Lloyd Garrison, who had recently violated his principles by rooting for the Mexican army, seemed disappointed in the conferences and said "they were characterized by great timidity." Nevertheless, these conferences first opened discussion of some of the most important ideas of the twentieth century including the League of Nations and the European Union.

In July 1848, with the Boston Clique still reeling from the February Treaty of Guadalupe Hidalgo, five women had tea in the home of Mary Ann McClintock in Waterloo, upstate New York. The house was also a station for fugitive slaves on the Underground Railroad. Her husband, Thomas, ran a store that only sold free-labor products. They also raised money for relief for the Irish famine. They were joined by Jane Hunt, who had just given birth to a daughter; Elizabeth Cady Stanton; and Lucretia Mott and her sister Martha Wright. The five resolved that they would hold a two-day women's rights convention in July at the Wesleyan Chapel on Fall Street in Seneca Falls, four miles from Waterloo. The Wesleyan Chapel had broken away from the Methodist Church to take a stand on abolition.

This was not a Boston event. Susan B. Anthony did not attend, though her mother and sister did. Maria Child was trying to stay away from activism. Margaret Fuller was in Italy. Frederick Douglass did attend; by this time, he had left Boston and was living in nearby Rochester. But for progressive women like Anthony and Child, this meeting would have an impact on the rest of their lives because it set the agenda for women for the rest of the nineteenth century.

About three hundred men and women attended. They issued a Declaration of Sentiments, modeled on the Declaration of Independence—"all men and women are created equal"—which served as the founding document of the American women's rights movement. Demands for equality in education, marriage, and jobs all passed unanimously. The only issue of controversy—ironically the one by which Seneca Falls would later be known—was the right of women to vote. Many women thought this was too ambitious a goal and would cause the entire movement to collapse. Some of the more militant women, such as Lucretia Mott, refused to support the measure. In the end, the vote for women's suffrage carried with the help of Frederick Douglass, who called it "simple justice." Douglass had always seen the connection between women's rights and Black rights. Both were being denied the full rights of citizenship. He remained an outspoken advocate for women's rights for the rest of his life.

Douglass had left Boston because he had split with Garrison. The breakup had the emotional weight of a sad and angry divorce. Lloyd had been Frederick's inspiration. Frederick had been Lloyd's most-admired lieutenant. They had spent endless months together traveling in North America and in Europe, speaking on the cause. The speeches were arranged to play to each other's strengths. The Lloyd-and-Frederick show was the best act in abolitionism. The split had numerous causes, and historians have struggled to sort out how it came to pass that these two friends and colleagues, who had once so admired each other, reached a point where they were not speaking. Perhaps the root of it was two men of great accomplishment with enormous egos.

From 1845 to 1847, Douglass was in England and Ireland. Even before he left in 1845 his celebrity was rapidly growing. The publication of his *Narrative* in 1845 made him not only the most famous Black man in America, but one of the most famous Americans. The book sold five thousand copies in its first four months and continued at an even faster pace. Wendell Phillips was the first to dub him "a lion" and the title stuck throughout his lifetime, and a century and a half later, Barack Obama referred to him as a lion. He looked like a lion in his many photographs. Massively attended farewell ceremonies were held for him at the Lyceum Hall in his hometown of Lynn and in his earlier hometown of New Bedford. He was greeted in England and later Ireland as a major American celebrity. Abolitionists feared that with his fame he was at even greater risk back in America. British Quakers found his southern owner and paid him £150, which would be almost $3,000 today, for Douglass's freedom. He had been functioning as a freeman, but this legal document would become significant in America.

Douglass pondered whether there was something more he could do with his increased fame. Life in America was insular. Americans seldom went to Europe. New Englanders seldom left New England. It was an adventure to go to New York. That he had standing in Europe made an important impression on Douglass. He was fascinated by the political upheavals of Europe in 1848. He began to see his cause as part of something larger in the world. Like David Child and Lloyd Garrison, becoming an international figure changed his perspective. He needed to do more when he went back to America.

British admirers encouraged him to return to America and start his own paper. They raised money to buy him a printing press and other equipment.

As was his custom, Douglass consulted Garrison and the Boston Clique and, to his surprise, he was told it was a bad idea. Garrison was emphatically opposed. They felt that it would take him away from speaking engagements, which was his real talent. Some historians have suggested that Garrison did not want competition for *The Liberator* but Garrison had always been supportive of attempts to launch a Black press. The four previous attempts at publishing a Black paper had all failed and he believed Douglass's would also fail. Douglass told his friend he had dropped the plan, though that wasn't true.

Garrison and Douglass went to Ohio on tour, after which Douglass went to Rochester to set up his press. Garrison was furious that Douglass had never said a word to him about his plan. Garrison said that this "grieves me at the heart."

In Rochester, a town of 50,000 on the Erie Canal and a major stop for fugitive slaves, Douglass began publishing the *North Star*, with the slogan on the masthead, "Right is of no color and no sex." He had never edited a paper, and for a time William Nell, who had gained experience on *The Liberator*, moved up to run the *North Star*.

A major backer was Gerrit Smith, one of the wealthiest abolitionists. Smith lived in nearby Peterboro, which was named after his father. Gerrit was a hypochondriac whose desk was filled with pills and potions, and he frequently predicted his impending death. He was a dedicated abolitionist and usually, but not always, a nonresistant. His father, Peter Smith Sr., who made a fortune from furs with John Jacob Astor, left his entire fortune to Gerrit. Despite his eccentricities, Gerrit was more stable than the other sons, Peter Jr., who lived with alcoholism, or Adolph, who ended up being institutionalized.

The free Black community of the 1840s had been increasingly contemplating violence, and Douglass had been one of its strongest opponents. At the 1843 National Convention of Colored Citizens in Buffalo, the New York minister Henry Highland Garnet delivered an address that he titled "Call to Rebellion." He was Douglass's age and, like him, an escaped slave from Maryland. The Convention was part of a decades-old and growing movement of "negro conventions." Originally the movement espoused Garrisonian nonresistance, but it had started slipping away from this position. Garnet said that Black people had to act by themselves to end slavery. He advocated armed rebellion, saying that nonviolence would be preferable but would not succeed.

In Buffalo, Frederick Douglass famously argued against Garnet's ideas. The convention had a vote on a call for armed rebellion, unheard of for a major abolitionist group, and it failed nineteen to eighteen. The convention did toss aside the nonresistant idea of refusing electoral politics, voting instead to support the Liberty Party. The only two votes against this resolution came from Douglass and Charles Remond.

Garnet was from New York, home of the least nonresistant abolitionist group, while New England had the most. When Douglass started the *North Star*, the paper was clearly nonresistant, though, like other nonresistant New Englanders, he believed that if slaveholders never relented, a violent slave revolt would be the inescapable consequence.

In the late 1840s Douglass was still speaking at Black gatherings about nonviolence. He was not the only prominent nonviolent Black activist. William Wells Brown, an escaped slave who became a Garrisonian in New England and who would later write the first novel by an African American, *Clotel*, in 1853, was part of the American delegation to the International Peace Congress held in Paris in 1849. He spoke of peaceful means as the only possibility for emancipation.

Songs of nonviolence were still being sung, such as James Russell Lowell's 1849 song:

Friends of Freedom! ye who stand
With no weapon in your hand,
Save a purpose stern and grand,
To set all men free . . .

But in the 1850s, driving deeper the wedge between Frederick and Lloyd, Douglass started believing that one possibility for nonviolent abolition was participation in electoral politics. Gerrit Smith, who seemed to skip from one idea to another, around 1850 abandoned nonresistance for political abolition, using politics. As Douglass recruited small checks from Smith to support his paper,

Smith recruited Douglass's support for his new political movement with ties to the Liberty Party. Nell too was being pulled into Smith's political abolitionism. In 1850 he ran for the Massachusetts legislature on a Liberty Party ticket and lost.

An increasing number of Garrisonian nonresistants were being drawn toward politics. In the 1840s they supported the Liberty Party as a response to Texas annexation. Elizabeth Cady Stanton's husband, Henry Stanton, onetime editor of *The Liberator*, abandoned his Garrisonian roots and formed the Free Soil Party from supporters of the Liberty Party. In the 1840s declared abolitionists started to gain seats in the House of Representatives. The first abolitionist elected to the Senate was Samuel P. Chase, New England–born but representing Ohio, in 1848. In 1850 Henry Stanton, who was widely admired as an orator, was elected to the New York Senate for the Free Soil Party.

In 1851, as the Free Soil Party was turning into the Republican Party, Charles Sumner was elected US Senator from Massachusetts. He was only forty years old. Theodore Parker, on Sumner's election, wrote to him, "You told me once that you were in morals, not politics. Now I hope that you will show that you are still in morals, although in politics. I hope that you will be the *senator with a conscience*."

Despite now being a senator, Sumner remained Vice President of the American Peace Society. Garrison said this was an unsustainable contradiction. In 1832 Prussian general Carl von Clausewitz wrote *On War*, a book still read in military academies around the world. Clausewitz wrote, "War is a mere continuation of policy by other means." Garrison probably didn't read it, but he would not have disagreed. He believed war was an option that policymakers would not rule out and being a nonviolent elected official was an inherent contradiction.

Douglass, putting the rules of nonresistance aside, welcomed Sumner's new position of power. But the Boston Clique—all of Douglass's old friends and comrades-in-arms such as Wendell Phillips and Stephen and Abby Kelley Foster—were now denouncing Douglass. Douglass was particularly furious that the Clique's Black members, such as Charles Lenox Remond, had turned against him. Though they had worked closely in Boston and Douglass even named a son after Remond, Remond had always nursed a grudge against Douglass, believing he had pushed him aside in the Garrison organization. But eventually Douglass even railed against Nell, who had come to work with him but stayed loyal to Garrison. Remond said that abolitionists were being too gentle with Douglass, "handling him with kid gloves."

Garrison was annoyed at all those who left his circle for politics. He said it was "contemptible" and "ludicrous." He said that running for office was "folly, presumption, almost unequalled infatuation." Entering electoral politics could mean more power in Washington, but it also might mean drifting away from nonviolence. Sumner would soon discover this reality.

Dialogue was becoming increasingly vitriolic. Garrison accused Douglass of using violent rhetoric. Douglass insisted that he was still a man of peace. But it was undeniable that his rhetoric was changing. In 1848 he wrote in the *North Star*, "Slavery will be attacked in its stronghold—the compromises of the Constitution, and the cry of disunion shall be more fearlessly proclaimed, till slavery be abolished, the Union dissolved, or the sun of this guilty nation must go down in blood."

The central portrait in this wood engraving from 1858 shows Anthony Burns when he was twenty-four years old, after he was freed.

Twelve

1850—

FUGITIVES

Oppression makes a wise man mad.
—Frederick Douglass, July 5, 1852

B y 1850 the United States was a completely divided country. It was a land of cynicism with little common ground. The dream of the Founding Fathers of a United States seemed shattered. The North and South could not even agree on a Thanksgiving holiday. It was a New England holiday sometimes more popular than Christmas, which the Childs found a bit Catholic. This was purely theirs.

Thanksgiving was Maria Child's favorite holiday. According to biographer Carolyn Karcher, it was her only happy childhood memory. Maria's parents always threw a feast in their large kitchen for the bakery workers, the sawyer, the washerwoman—all the working people. They would make chicken pies, pumpkin pies, and copious amounts of donuts. The workers were sent home with pies and, of course, a lot of crackers. Maria and

David never had such large staffs to entertain, but she would still bake an occasional Thanksgiving pumpkin pie. When she lived in Boston, she had children to play with—Helen and Lloyd Garrison's five and Sarah and Francis Shaw's four daughters and son Robert. She had fewer children around her in New York, but in 1845, during the period when she was trying to be more literary and less political, she wrote a series of poems for children, *Flowers for Children*, which included a Thanksgiving poem that became very popular in New England with the famous opening line, "Over the river and through the wood / To Grandfather's house we go." The closing line was, "Hurra for the pumpkin pie!" This is her celebrated pumpkin and squash pie recipe:

> *For common family pumpkin pies, three eggs do very well to a quart of milk. Stew your pumpkin, and strain it through a sieve, or colander. Take out the seeds, and pare the pumpkin, or squash, before you stew it; but do not scrape the inside; the part nearest the seed is the sweetest part of the squash. Stir in the stewed pumpkin, till it is so thick as you can stir it round rapidly and easily. If you want to make your pie richer, make it thinner, and add another egg. One egg to a quart of milk makes very decent pies. Sweeten it to your taste, with molasses or sugar; some pumpkins require more sweetening than others. Two tea-spoonfuls of salt; two great spoonfuls of sifted cinnamon; one great spoonful of ginger. Ginger will answer very well alone for spice, if you use enough of it. The outside of a lemon grated in is nice. The more eggs, the better the pie; some put an egg to a gill of milk. They should bake from forty to fifty minutes, and even ten minutes longer, if very deep.*

To New Englanders, the holiday celebrated those first brave men and women who came to America seeking freedom. Sarah Josepha Hale, a New Englander born in New Hampshire, a donor to the Bunker Hill Monument and editor of America's most popular magazine, *Godey's Lady's Book*, was Thanksgiving's great champion. Starting in 1846, the year after Maria Child's poem, and continuing relentlessly year after year, Hale campaigned to make Thanksgiving a national holiday. Southerners, led by tobacco-chewing Virginia governor Henry Wise, who would later ask for a death sentence for John Brown, vehemently objected, saying it was one more attempt by New Englanders to impose their values on the South.

But in the North, especially since the Treaty of Guadalupe Hidalgo, more and more were questioning America's founding myths of freedom. It was a perfect time for Nathaniel Hawthorne, a writer with caustic wit and a flair for satire. Ticknor and Fields convinced him to develop his short story about the Puritans that he had been toying with at the West Street bookstore into a full novel, and in 1850 *The Scarlet Letter* was published. Today it is taught as a book about guilt, remorse, and repentance, but in 1850, it was setting the record straight about the people Hawthorne called, with an unmistakable sneer, "our great forefathers." While Sarah Josepha Hale was trying to push the nation into celebrating these brave ancestors, Hawthorne revealed our great forefathers as cruel and hypocritical. He described the times Hale was celebrating as "those dreary old times" and wrote of "Puritans being of the most intolerant brood that ever lived." Hawthorne even asserted that the Puritans were too grim to know how to celebrate a holiday. If Hawthorne had it right, the first Thanksgiving would not have been much fun.

What did the Americans of 1850 think of this attack on their forefathers? It was the biggest bestseller in American literary history up to that time. Some religious leaders in both the North and South called for banning the book because Hawthorne was sympathetic to Hester Prynne, an adulteress, whom he describes physically in the same way he once described Margaret Fuller—with "dark and rich hair." In fact, in 1850 it was rumored that Margaret's child, like Hester's, was conceived out of wedlock. It is not certain if these rumors inspired Hawthorne or if Hawthorne's book inspired the rumors.

For 1850, there was a remarkable consensus on this book. To southerners, it confirmed what they had always thought of Puritans, while in New England, it was even hailed by transcendentalists. Theodore Parker persuaded George Bailey Loring, a well-regarded doctor, to write an article for the *Massachusetts Quarterly Review* ensconcing Hester Prynne as a transcendentalist heroine for going her own way and rising above the dictates of a narrow-minded society and rejecting Puritan morality. Loring wrote of this Puritan code, "We gain nothing by this hardness."

Only the author's hometown of Salem condemned the book for its depiction of Puritans. One article attacked the "malignant Hawthorne" for his "cold and heartless sneer." Maybe, but it was a well-received sneer in 1850. The times were ripe for sneering.

Some compromise had to be worked out to bring peace in 1850 to two irreconcilable sides. The annexation of Texas and the Mexican War exploded the slavery issue. It opened a huge area to be divided into states that would be either slave or free. Many Americans, not just abolitionists, wanted no expansion of slavery. During the Mexican War, a Pennsylvania congressman, David Wilmot, introduced the Wilmot Proviso, which would have banned slavery in all the new states. Congressmen such as Abraham Lincoln, who were not abolitionists but disliked slavery, voted for the proviso. So did Horace Mann. It repeatedly passed in the House but was defeated in the Senate, which was controlled by southern slave states.

Another compromise had to be found. Henry Clay of Virginia wrote the Compromise of 1850. The compromise was to allow Texas to be a slave state in exchange for California being free. They each were to have four electoral votes. Other territories were to be decided by "popular sovereignty," meaning that the settlers would vote on the issue when they were ready for statehood.

Many northerners might have accepted the Compromise as a compromise if it had not included the Fugitive Slave Act. If the slaveholders of the South had wanted to undermine the notion of moral suasion in Boston, if they had wanted to stir the Massachusetts citizenry to abolition, if they had wanted to move abolitionists to both physical and political action, they could not have done better than the Fugitive Slave Act of 1850.

This law provided that police and federal Marshals could be ordered to capture slaves found in a free state and return them to the slaveholders. The accused slaves were not to be granted any due process of law, not even an opportunity to prove that they were actually free. No person of color was safe.

Historians argue over how many slaves escaped to freedom between 1835 and the Civil War; estimates range from 60,000 to 150,000, or possibly more.

Slaveholders believed they were defending their legal property rights. It was about returning their lost property. Crazy

Abigail Folsom might well have screamed, "Capitalism!" Northerners saw this new law as an unconstitutional infringement on state rights, and due process of law, and a takeover of northern law enforcement by southern slaveholders.

Massachusetts and other states passed laws restricting the ability of Marshals to capture escaped slaves and banning the use of state officials or state jails. Maria Child wrote a pamphlet asserting that there was "a duty of disobedience to the Fugitive Slave Act."

A large angry crowd gathered in Faneuil Hall to hear the nation's most famous fugitive slave, Frederick Douglass, legally no longer a fugitive, called back from Rochester, as he put it, "in behalf of a suffering and terrified population." Now Douglass and Boston were reunited, though he and Garrison were still not speaking to each other. Douglass, the former nonresistant, declared that there would be blood in the streets before Black people allowed the return of anyone to slavery.

Boston lawyers studied the new laws and how to fight them. Boston streets were made for civil disobedience. A few main arteries for large demonstrations were surrounded by ganglia of narrow, twisting streets that provided good escape routes. The streets and parks of Boston were bustling with vigilantes searching for "slave-hunters." They were to be found mostly in the few straight avenues and parks since only Bostonians could navigate the chaotic side streets. If a slave hunter could be located, he could be driven out of town. Slave hunters grabbed people on the street, in bars, or in other public places, but they did not dare invade private spaces. Private homes on both sides of Beacon Hill and throughout the city provided shelter to fugitives. With slave hunters stalking Black people and abolitionists stalking slave hunters, Boston was becoming a dangerous place.

In 1850, Rome was not having a good year either. The Roman Revolution had failed, and Margaret Fuller, at age forty, decided to return to America with her husband and son. It was a sign of the times that her Boston friends, including Ralph Waldo Emerson, Maria Child, and William Henry Channing, wrote letters arguing that this was not a good time to be in America and she would be better off staying in Italy. She dismissed their pleas, saying she was only going to stay for three or four years and then go back. She had written a book on the Roman Revolution for which she wanted to find an American publisher.

In serious financial difficulties, Margaret's family booked a cargo ship rather than a passenger boat. The passenger ships had the latest in navigational equipment. Cargo ships were more rustic and dangerous. But they selected a ship and interviewed the captain, a seasoned Maine seaman, and they had confidence in him. The ship had twenty-two passengers and, ironically, was carrying, along with slabs of marble, a marble statue of the recently deceased John C. Calhoun, the great champion of slavery and southern interests, to be installed prominently in Charleston.

Unfortunately, early in the voyage, the captain died of smallpox and a very inexperienced first mate was left in charge. Almost home, their ship was hit by a freak storm off of Fire Island, New York. It was a well-traveled, well-charted passage, and the ship should not have wrecked. Even when it did run aground on a shoal, the passengers waded the shallow passage to nearby land about fifty feet away. All of the passengers, officers, and crew survived. But Margaret, with a lifelong fear of water, her family, and their cook, Celeste, logically waited to be rescued. Inexplicably, no one from the crowd that collected on the shore tried to get a boat or rescue them. Margaret and her husband did not know that when the ship hit the shoal, the Calhoun statue and other weighty marble slabs burst a hole in the hull and the ship began to come apart in the surf. The family drowned.

At Emerson's urging, Thoreau went to the site to try to find their bodies and possibly her book manuscript. But he had no success.

In 1851 Lloyd Garrison kept his readers focused on the fugitive slave crisis. By the end of the year, he had reported on nineteen cases of Black people arrested in the North and forcibly returned to slavery in the South.

The Fugitive Slave Act was spreading abolitionism, but destroying nonviolence. Dr. Samuel Howe, who had not participated in abolitionist functions, now became very active, a speaker at meetings and an advocate of violence. Higginson, who did not believe in nonresistance, also became a radical abolitionist because of the Fugitive Slave Act. In Medford, there was a new activism from the wealthiest citizen, the husband of Maria Child's niece Mary, George Luther Stearns. Despite his radical wife, he seemed a conservative business type in suits from his London tailor, though a long, curly beard that covered his chest made him look like a well-dressed poodle. He said the beard was to protect him from his chronic bronchitis. But then he changed. According to his son, "The fugitive slave law affected Mr. Stearns like the blow of an assailant." He bought a revolver and declared that he would never let a fugitive be taken from his property. His Medford mansion became a refuge and a station on the Underground Railroad.

Henry Wright, a Garrisonian nonresistant minister who, according to popular rumor, had lost his parish for the unclerical act of swimming across the Connecticut River, reacted to the 1850 law by telling his followers to arm themselves with "deadly weapons" and "inflict death with his own hand" on anyone who attempted to kidnap an escaped slave. Theodore Parker armed himself with a sword and loaded pistol and organized mobs to drive slave hunters out of Boston.

In Boston, posters were put up warning Black people to "keep a sharp lookout for kidnappers" and "to avoid conversing with the watchmen and police officers."

Charles Hobson came to Boston hunting for his escaped slave, Henry Langhorn. Langhorn reported to the Massachusetts Anti-Slavery Society office that he had seen Hobson and feared he was in Boston to take him. The Boston Vigilance Committee checked Boston hotels and soon located Hobson. They quickly moved Langhorn to the home of Francis Jackson on 31 Hollis Street. Jackson was a close friend and avid supporter of Lloyd Garrison. He had been working with the Vigilance Committee, which had been founded in 1841 to protect escaped slaves. Along with Jackson, Francis Shaw was one of the primary funders of the committee. Howe became head of the committee. They operated until the Civil War, and in twenty years, they helped hundreds of escapees, many of whom had arrived in Boston Harbor as stowaways.

Hobson placed ads in the Boston newspapers offering a reward for the capture of Langhorn and included a description of him. The Vigilance Committee responded with their own ad following Hobson's format. It warned that Charles Hobson, a Virginia slave owner, was trying to kidnap his escaped slave; the kidnapper was staying at the Tremont Hotel. It also gave a physical description of him and the clothes that he wore. Hobson, knowing how disliked slavecatchers were in Boston, rapidly departed from town.

Massachusetts courts were often sympathetic to fugitive slaves, but they also tried to enforce existing laws. Once arrested and identified as fugitive slaves, even if they were freed by the court, slavecatchers could grab them again at the court and invent a new charge. The committee had to slip them out of court, out of town, perhaps out of the country. Two Black women, Eliza Small and Polly Ann Bates, were brought before Judge Lemuel Shaw (Melville's father-in-law) and the courtroom was filled with abolitionists, mostly Black women. When Judge Shaw freed the two women on a writ of habeas corpus (an assertion that the charge had no legal standing), the slavecatcher moved forward to press a new charge. But the abolitionists grabbed the two women first, blocked the slavecatcher, and sent the two to safety.

In 1851, Boston law officers entered a coffee house and arrested a waiter named Shadrach, claiming he was an escaped Virginia slave, and took him to a courtroom. A large crowd of Black people entered the courtroom, putting on a show of how racists imagined Black people to act, being boisterous, laughing, pushing, shoving, and acting silly, until Shadrach was lost in the crowd. They slipped him out and sent him to safety in Canada. Garrison wrote of the incident in *The Liberator*, "a sudden rush of a score or two of unarmed friends of equal liberty—an uninjurious deliverance of the oppressed out of the hand of the oppressor." Daniel Webster, who was Secretary of State, denounced the action. Henry Clay called for a toughening of his Fugitive Slave Act.

Abolitionists knew that their victories would be few. The city was flooded with slave hunters because, for the southern slaveholders, the ultimate victory would be to bring one back from Boston. Wendell Phillips said, "All they want is one from Boston to show the discontented ones at home that it can be done."

Later in 1851, Thomas Sims, an escaped bricklayer from Savannah, was arrested on a spurious charge of disturbing the peace. Once in custody he was turned over to federal Marshals as a runaway. Since Massachusetts did not allow its jails to be used for holding accused fugitives, the slim twenty-three-year-old was kept under guard in the courtroom.

A meeting was held at the Tremont Temple, a Greek Revival-style theater that had been converted into a Baptist church with a racially integrated congregation. Horace Mann agreed to lead the meeting at the Tremont Temple, as his predecessor, Adams, had on numerous occasions. Mann's only condition was that the meeting not propose violent and illegal actions. He had imagined a more tranquil meeting. Theodore Parker spurred on an angry crowd, many of whom had come from rural Massachusetts. The meeting settled on the idea of storming the courthouse the following morning and freeing Sims.

When a boisterous horde arrived the next morning, they found the courthouse sealed off with chains and ropes and guarded not only by what appeared to be the entire Boston police force but also paid toughs from the waterfront.

The public was not allowed to enter, and even Judge Shaw, aged but still of upright posture, was forced to squat beneath a chained barrier to enter his court. Vigils were held at the courthouse and there were rallies on the Common. Wendell Phillips, one of the most resolute nonresistants of the Boston Clique, told the crowd that Boston would be disgraced if they did not block any attempt to remove Sims.

Higginson, growing more violent by the day, met at the shabby office of *The Liberator* with Stearns, Parker, and Howe—men who never had a strong attachment to nonviolence. They considered either an armed assault on the courthouse or hiring privateers to overtake the ship taking Sims back to Savannah. They had the money and the will to do something. In an earlier time, Lloyd Garrison would have shouted denunciations of such plans, but now he simply did not want to be seen listening to them. He removed himself to his type bench and composed an editorial while the others had their meeting. In the end, they could not decide on a plan of action.

Judge Shaw issued a "certificate of removal" and Sims was led down State Street to the Long Wharf in the center of a square of three hundred policemen armed with battle sabers. Behind them marched Parker, Wendell Phillips, and others carrying a black-draped coffin.

Though Sims had been taken away in tears, the *Boston Daily Mail* speciously reported that he had been singing "Carry Me Back to Old Virginia." When Sims arrived in Savannah, he was publicly whipped—thirty-nine lashes on his bare back. After that, many in Massachusetts were outraged, and it is not a coincidence that two weeks after Sims was shipped back to Savannah, the Massachusetts legislature voted Sumner United States Senator—Massachusetts's first abolitionist senator. (At the time, state legislatures and not popular votes elected senators.)

Each fugitive case hardened abolitionist positions and weakened nonviolence. The lesson for abolitionists from the Sims case was that official Boston, the city, the courts, and the police sided with the enemy. Frederick Douglass wrote that "Daniel Webster has at last obtained from Boston . . . a living sacrifice to appease the slave god of the American Union." For abolitionists, belonging to that union seemed increasingly questionable.

Slave owners were invigorated by the belief that federal law was on their side. Frederick Douglass in 1851 in the *North Star* predicted that "the land will be filled with violence and blood till this law is repealed."

In 1854, an escaped Virginia slave, Anthony Burns, a tailor and ministerial student, was arrested in Boston. Burns, like many of the Boston refugees, had stowed away on a Boston-bound ship. He worked for several months in a clothing store and was then detected by a letter he wrote home. Sims had been caught the same way. This started to look like a Sims rerun. Burns too was locked in the courthouse, the building wrapped in chains and surrounded by police. President Pierce sent two artillery companies, a detachment of cavalry as well as marines. A ship docked in the harbor, ready to take Burns back. Robert Morris, along with Richard Henry Dana Jr., who changed maritime law with his exposé *Two Years Before the Mast*, were Burns's attorneys. Morris may have been the first Black attorney in the United States (in 1848, Morris, along with Charles Sumner, had taken a case challenging segregated schools to the Massachusetts Supreme Court; they lost, but it was the first legal challenge to school segregation in Massachusetts).

Whittier proposed gathering huge numbers from outside the city to nonviolently march on Boston. Many of the about sixty members of the Vigilance Committee, all men, also nonviolent, agreed. They wanted to follow the man claiming to be Burns's master, Charles Suttle, around town, pointing him out, and shouting at him and encouraging a crowd to join in, until he was driven out of town like Charles Hobson a few years earlier.

Higginson believed such nonviolent approaches would never work. He argued with Parker and Wendell Phillips, who liked Whittier's proposal. Huge numbers, unarmed, would block the courthouse until the guards were forced to surrender Burns. Higginson had no patience for this plan. Meanwhile, some two thousand people had packed into Faneuil Hall to hear speech after speech by abolitionists, mostly not nonviolent in tone. Sam Howe made a speech in which he said, "The time has come to declare and demonstrate that no slave hunter can carry his prey from the Commonwealth of Massachusetts."

Rhetoric grew increasingly violent and eventually about two hundred men marched to the courthouse. Higginson had planned to give a signal and lead the crowd. But amid the chaos and shouting, no signal could be heard. Phillips took to the podium and suggested that they attack at daybreak. Then men shouted that the attack was beginning. It seemed that no one was in control anymore. The crowd pushed their way out of the hall and Higginson struggled to get to the front of it. He finally managed to arrive at the courthouse with a group of Black men who, with a beam as a battering ram, broke down the door. Higginson made it into the courthouse but was beaten back out, receiving a facial wound that he proudly displayed for some time after. In the melee, one guard was killed, which frightened Higginson's mob, and they retreated.

The police had been ready for Higginson, whose assault had been announced hours in advance. Maria Child, who traditionally abhorred violence, complained that the abolitionists had forewarned the enemy with too much rhetoric in Faneuil Hall instead of quickly attacking the courthouse. "If they had only struck when the iron was hot," she wrote to Francis Shaw.

A week later, an estimated fifty thousand Bostonians, more than a third of the city's population, lined the streets to witness Anthony Burns being marched in shackles to the waterfront to be shipped back to slavery. But he did not stay in the South. Abolitionists paid $1,300 for him, the equivalent of about $50,000 today. Within a year, he was back in Boston. He studied for the ministry in Ohio and moved on to safety in Canada, where he tragically died of tuberculosis at the age of twenty-eight.

Wendell Phillips said that white people should remain nonviolent, but if a Black person felt threatened by a federal Marshal, he should "feel justified by using the law of God and man in shooting that officer."

Only a few now held to the code of nonresistance. Frederick Douglass wrote an editorial: "Is it Right and Wise to Kill a Kidnapper?" He argued that self-defense is a natural right and that if government failed to protect people, "friends" could exercise their rights to do whatever was necessary.

In the Boston Clique, some were seeing the wisdom in voting. In 1855, in his revised autobiography, Frederick Douglass wrote that "to abstain from voting, was to refuse to exercise a legitimate and powerful means for abolishing slavery."

The Fugitive Slave Act had not worked. Only a small fraction of the escaped slaves were sent back. In 1850 a line had been drawn. Not only were northerners outraged and embracing abolition as never before, but southern slaveholders were infuriated by the northern response. Ten years later when southern states were seceding from the Union, some states listed among their reasons the refusal of the North to enforce the Fugitive Slave Act.

Senator Charles Sumner, photograph by Mathew Brady.

Thirteen

1856—

THE PRACTICE WAR

*Of what value or utility are the principles of peace
and forgiveness, if we may repudiate them in the
hour of peril and suffering.*

—William Lloyd Garrison to his sons, 1858

In 1856 the divided United States seemed on the edge of a violent split. It had been clearly headed that way for a number of years. In 1854 in his new book *Walden*, Thoreau wrote, "Could a greater miracle take place than for us to look through each other's eyes for an instant?" In the 1850s that would be a miracle.

By 1852 there was already not a lot of fence-sitting. You were either on one side or the other. The transcendentalists admired and praised Hawthorne's new novel, and Hester Prynne, the heroine, was the embodiment of Emerson's principle of self-reliance. But it was becoming clear with his next book, a biography of Franklin Pierce, that their friend Hawthorne was not on their side.

Frank Pierce, as Hawthorne knew him, was a classmate of Hawthorne at Bowdoin College, which at the time had about a dozen men in a class doing everything together. Pierce, unlike Hawthorne and most of his friends, was a political conservative. He built the right-wing New Hampshire Democratic Party. Though a New Englander, Pierce often expressed his antipathy for abolitionists, who he claimed were destabilizing the country. Hawthorne wrote a laudatory biography of his friend Frank for his 1852 presidential campaign.

Most of Hawthorne's Boston friends were not sure whether to respond with anger or ridicule. Horace Mann, married to the sister of Hawthorne's wife, said, "If he makes out Pierce to be a great man or a brave man, it will be the greatest work of fiction he ever wrote." Higginson later wrote, "It had always been painful to me that he [Hawthorne], alone among the prominent literary men of New England, should be persistently arrayed on what seemed to me the wrong side." Higginson blamed it on his friendship with Pierce.

Another Bowdoin classmate was Calvin Stowe, who married abolitionist Harriet Beecher, author of *Uncle Tom's Cabin*. Pierce at one point said he got through college by cheating off of Stowe. Calvin also spoke well of their classmate, Frank. Maria Child, responding to Hawthorne's praise of Pierce, wrote in a letter to a friend, "If I were his wife, I'd sue for divorce."

Hawthorne praised Pierce's military service in the Mexican War, avoiding the frequent suggestions of cowardice from the battles he avoided by claiming injuries from his horse. But even if he was heroic in the Mexican War, that war was a disgrace to many in Massachusetts. Pierce won by a landslide, but Massachusetts and Vermont were two of only four states that voted against him.

Pierce thought he could bring peace by denouncing quarrelsome abolitionists and placating slaveholders. Sending federal troops to Boston in 1854 was not even the worst of the Pierce administration. Pierce's backing of an unsuccessful attempt to take the slave colony of Cuba from Spain and make it a slave state seemed to clarify which side he was on. In 1853 Pierce sent Hawthorne to England with a cushy diplomatic posting that allowed the author to miss the worst period of the Pierce presidency.

Garrison would have preferred for the abolitionist controversy to stay focused on the Fugitive Slave Act. But in 1854 the Kansas-Nebraska Act was passed, which stirred up even more anger and violence. It was the pet project of Illinois senator Stephen A. Douglas, who was mainly concerned with recognizing the territory of Nebraska so that a transcontinental railroad coming from the west coast could run through Nebraska to Iowa and make Chicago "the gateway to the west."

The Kansas-Nebraska Act once again raised the idea of popular sovereignty. Since 1820 it had been agreed that no territory above the parallel 36°30' north could allow slavery. It was part of the "compromise" that gave Missouri entry as a slave state. Now whether or not slavery would be legal in Kansas and Nebraska, above the line, would be decided by the settlers that lived there.

The anger this produced reshaped American politics. The Whig Party, which was a major political party built on opposition to the Mexican War, split apart. The Whigs had tried to straddle the slavery issue, and this was no longer possible in the 1850s. Southern proslavery Whigs left and joined the Democrats. Northern antislavery Whigs left and formed the

Republican Party. Both abolitionists and proslavery forces tried to get as many of their people into Kansas as they could. As abolitionists moved to Kansas, guerrilla fighters, known as ruffians, moved in from Missouri, using armed violence to push them out. The abolitionists, who had claimed to be nonresistants, armed themselves to fight back. It became a war. Pierce backed the Missourians, but government was not controlling either side.

Though the Boston Clique was largely throwing Kansas its support, Garrison was not enthusiastic about the fight. Most of the free settlers were not antislavery abolitionists in general, they only stood for antislavery in Kansas. Some of the settlers tried to bar free Blacks from coming to Kansas. Some wanted a white-only free state. Garrison criticized "the longitude and latitude of compromise."

Northerners collected clothing, food, and supplies for the people they called the northern emigrants. In one year, the National Kansas Committee shipped 762 boxes to Kansas, a large number of them from Massachusetts. People from Massachusetts had moved to Kansas and had their homes torn down. A few had been killed. Stories from Kansas of invasion, violence, and civil war filled the newspapers. Even *The Liberator* started running headlines such as "Invasion of Kansas" and "The Gathering Storm" and "The Kansas Inquisition." And in June 1856, there was the headline "Civil War In Kansas."

John Brown, once a dismissed eccentric, was starting to be taken seriously among his fellow abolitionists. Kansas was fertile ground for Brown's violence. His five sons were already in Kansas, and Brown was raising money for arms to go there and fight. Gerrit Smith held a convention in Syracuse that collected money from abolitionists for pistols and ammunition.

Boston abolitionists sent aid, not weapons, but some, especially transcendentalists, were sending arms. Brown was opening rifts in the movement. Parker declared that he would divert the funds for purchases for his library to buy Sharps rifles and ammunition for Kansas. Sharps rifles were expensive, state-of-the-art weapons valued because they loaded from the breech rather than the muzzle, and so could easily be reloaded on horseback.

Higginson visited Kansas and returned, likening it to the Battle of Bunker Hill. In New England, Bunker Hill was often a metaphor for permissible violence. He used the motto "peaceful if we can, forcibly if we must." But it was clear which approach he was backing, since he tried to gather support for sending an armed militia to fight in Kansas.

The Liberator sent a correspondent to Kansas, Charles Stearns, a distant relative of George Luther Stearns and a dedicated Garrisonian nonresistant. He was not what Garrison expected. From Kansas he wrote, "My non-resistance has at length yielded." He said he now carried weapons and stood guard duty, ready to kill. When admonished by Garrison, he argued that he was still opposed to killing a fellow human being, but he did not regard Missouri ruffians as human. He called them "drunken ourang-outangs." In addition to their brutality, they were hard drinkers, which was something Garrisonians associated with evil. Stearns claimed it was his "duty to aid in killing them off."

He beseeched fellow abolitionists to come to Kansas and join the fight. Not the only one, but one of the first, to declare the opening of the Civil War, he wrote of the fight in Kansas, "The war, if once commenced, will not, must not cease, until every slave throughout the Union is liberated." This was John Brown's idea as well, to start the Civil War in Kansas, and an increasing number of abolitionists were beginning to agree.

Lloyd Garrison stated that he would rather lose Kansas than abandon nonviolence. But even in the Boston Clique, there were few who agreed with him. Many of those calling for armed resistance, such as Higginson, had never been pacifist. Some, like Stearns and even Brown, had converted, and many, such as Maria Child, were struggling.

While David Child was working on getting Sharps rifles shipped to Kansas, Maria was up at night sewing and preparing aid packages for the abolitionists who had moved to Kansas. She was far from approving of John Brown's approach, but she did not agree with Garrison's idea that they should let Kansas go rather than be pulled into violence. She refuted the American Anti-Slavery Society's condemnation of the free state settlers taking up arms. She said the AASS position was "narrow and intolerant." She was angered by "the cruel outrages" of the Missouri ruffians and defended the abolitionists, even if violent. "I can never call those men murderers, who forsake home and kindred, and all that renders life agreeable, and with noble self-sacrifice go forth to suffer and to die in the cause of freedom."

Actually, despite the rhetoric and the arms shipments for free state settlers, most of the killing was done by the other side. Fifty-two died in Kansas in 1855 and 1856 and three-quarters of the deaths were Free-Staters. Twenty-eight of the Free-Staters that died were out-and-out murdered. Only eight on the proslavery side were murdered, and five of those were by John Brown and his sons in Pottawatomie. Brown was by far the single most violent abolitionist. Some abolitionists supported him, and many criticized him, but almost none joined him except for a small band of fighters.

Maria Child wanted to hold on to her principles of nonviolence, but she also wanted to see action taken. "Nothing suits my mood so well," she wrote Charles Sumner, "as Jeanne d'Arc's floating banner and consecrated sword."

In her 1856 short story, "The Kansas Emigrants," Maria wrote that "Human nature was goaded beyond endurance, and men were in the mood to do, or die."

Garrison tried to fight that mood. He and Adin Ballou revived the old New England Non-Resistance Society with a large, well-publicized conference. To all their customary Christian arguments, they added one that must have been shocking to New Englanders: they argued that Kansas was not worth sacrificing their principles. Neither of them thought the policies of the Free-Staters—"shuffling policy," Garrison called it—deserved a sacrifice of important ideals. In an attempt to expose the absurdity of sending armed combatants to Kansas, he said satirically why not get at the heart of the problem and launch a military invasion of the South? But, to his horror, he realized that not everyone thought that was a bad idea.

Then the violence spread beyond Kansas—to Washington, DC. On May 20, 1856, Senator Sumner delivered a speech in the Senate denouncing the brutish violence of the Missouri ruffians in Kansas and ridiculing Senator Stephen A. Douglas and South Carolina senator Andrew P. Butler, whom he likened to Don Quixote and Sancho Panza, for supporting the ruffians. After the speech, the Senate was emptying, and Sumner was seated, addressing at his desk copies of the speech to be mailed. South Carolina congressman Preston Brooks walked up to the seated Sumner and told him that his speech "is a libel to South Carolina and Mr. Butler, who is a relative of mine." He then took a heavy gold-headed cane and struck Sumner from behind, according to accounts, more than thirty times in the head and shoulders while Sumner tried to get out from behind the desk. He finally managed to pull the desk from its floor bolts and stand up, only to fall to the floor, lying in his blood.

Brooks, previously little known, was taking bows in the South and being presented with tokens of admiration from political and business groups, including a cane that said, "Hit him again."

Northerners were seeing something of the South they had not wanted to see. Frederick Douglass knew the South. In his autobiography, he wrote, "Everybody in the South wants the privilege of whipping somebody else." Were these the people they were to turn with moral suasion? In Boston and much of the North, it was thought that southerners were violent and cowardly and there was no possibility of reasoning with them. Garrison's Christian precept of returning evil with goodness was being replaced by evil for evil, which is the definition of war. The attack did much to promote the shipping of arms to Kansas and the pursuit of a Kansas war.

The attack infuriated John Brown, who was already looking for vengeance for some 750 red-shirted border ruffians carrying flags with such slogans as "The Supremacy of the white race," who rode into the Free-State capital of Lawrence. Finding that the abolitionists had fled, they destroyed homes and buildings. For Brown, the hacking murders in Pottawatomie were a direct response.

Despite her disdain for politics and politicians, Maria Child had followed Charles Sumner's career with great admiration. Three years earlier, in 1853, Maria had praised the senator's speech denouncing the Fugitive Slave Act. Sumner replied with a note acknowledging how much he had been influenced by her antislavery writing. Maria Child kept the letter among her most treasured possessions.

She said that when she learned of Sumner's beating, it made her physically ill. She wrote to Sarah Shaw that for several days she experienced "painful suffocation of the heart, alternating with painful throbbing of the brain." Typical of Child, she wanted to nurse Sumner but could not get away from Wayland, where she was nursing her elderly father.

She wrote to Lucretia Mott that it had been Kansas and the attack on Sumner that had recommitted her to "hunt the Demon Slavery with all the energy and all the activity I possess."

Part of her renewal was attending the 1856 New England Anti-Slavery Society meeting on Cornhill Street, famous for its bookstores and located near *The Liberator.* Listening to the speeches reenergized her. According to abolitionist Franklin Sanborn, Brown was also at the meeting and stormed out, snarling, "Talk! Talk! Talk!" Brown and Maria Child did not meet.

After the Sumner attack, she wrote to Sarah Shaw that this was the moment of crisis. "If the slave-power is checked now, it will never regain its strength. If it is not checked, civil war is inevitable, and with all my horror of bloodshed, I could be better resigned to that great calamity than to endure this tyranny that has so long trampled on us."

She was losing patience. She wrote to Lucy Osgood, a Medford woman twelve years older than Maria who had been a childhood mentor, "when this state of mind was rebuked by the remembrance of him who taught us to overcome evil only with good, I could do nothing better than groan out, in a tone of despairing reproach, 'How long, O Lord! how long?'"

If she was still trying to cling to nonviolence, she had abandoned the Garrisonian idea of nonparticipation. After the goals
of women had been declared at Seneca Falls, it was becoming
difficult for feminists to demand that women have the right to
vote while at the same time advocating refusal to vote. Maria had
moved past her hatred and distrust of politics and started to be
drawn in. This new interest was helping to heal a rift in her marriage. Like their friend Lloyd Garrison, Maria had always been
annoyed by David's interest in and even involvement in politics.
Now it was something David and Maria had in common as they
settled into a new life together in her father's house in Wayland,
a quiet town west of Boston.

A few of the Bostonians, including Ballou and Garrison,
held firmly to the principles of nonresistance. They refused to
participate in the political process, and they denounced the
Union and the Constitution. They believed the Constitution,
because it permitted slavery, was a proslavery document, though
others pointed out that it also gave Congress the right to abolish slavery. In 1845 Sumner had argued the point with Wendell
Phillips, saying that all constitutions "sanction what I consider
injustice and wrong." As an example, he cited the fact that they
all sanctioned war, "which is a sin as hateful & mischievous as
that of slavery."

In 1854 at a July 4 rally Garrison had burned a copy of the
Constitution, calling it "a covenant with death, and an agree-
ment with hell," and then added, "So perish all compromises
with tyranny! And let all people say, 'Amen.'" The crowd shouted
"Amen!" It was one of Garrison's most famous moments.

In 1856 Garrison went further, calling in *The Liberator* for a
dissolution of the Union:

We, therefore, believe that the time has come for a new ar-
rangement of elements so hostile, of interests so irreconcilable,
of institutions so incongruous; and we earnestly request Con-
gress, at its present session, to take such initiatory measures for
the speedy, peaceful, and equitable dissolution of the existing
Union as the exigencies of the case require.

He called on the South to "depend upon her own resources"
and understood, as most did, that the South depended on the
more developed northern economy. At the time of Garrison's
call in 1856, Maria Child wrote to Sarah Shaw, "For many
years, it has been a settled conviction in my mind that there is
no remedy for this, except Dissolution of the Union. But how
can it be dissolved? That is the question."

Higginson was committed to disunion, as was Thoreau, who
wrote in his journal, "My thoughts are murder to the State."

In the 1856 presidential campaign, Maria Child for the first
time backed a candidate. She was committed to the Republican
candidacy of California senator John C. Frémont. She wrote
to Sarah Shaw, "I never was bitten by politics before; but such
mighty issues are depending on this election that I cannot be
indifferent." She also wrote to her, "What a shame that women
can't vote," and expressed confidence that giving women the
right to vote would ensure Frémont's victory. Even Garrison
was supporting Frémont. It was a mark of the desperation of
the times that people such as Garrison and Child would support Frémont. As a Western explorer, he was held responsible
for the massacre of hundreds of Native Americans, and he had

also played a role in the Mexican War. Frémont, like fellow Republican Abraham Lincoln, was not an abolitionist but firmly resolved to not allow any expansion of slavery. That was enough for abolitionists to cling to. Many abolitionists—and many slaveholders—were convinced that such a man in the White House would end slavery. They were right, except they had the wrong Republican.

Maria described to Sarah Shaw how they had carefully lifted into a carriage and slowly driven her invalid father, Convers Sr., who had cast his first vote for George Washington, to the voting place where he deposited his vote for Frémont with a trembling hand.

It was generally agreed that Pierce had been a disaster in his handling, or not handling, of Kansas, and the Democratic Party refused to nominate him for a second term and instead chose James Buchanan, who was open to the expansion of slavery. Though Frémont swept New England and won other northern states, the Democrats swept the South and won five northern states, including Frémont's California, to win the election.

When Brown went to Boston in 1857, he stayed with Waldo Emerson in Concord. This was an odd pairing. Emerson was one of the leading intellectuals in America, heading a philosophical movement. Even his friends sometimes confessed that they found transcendentalism hard to follow. Brown was a man of action who disliked intellectualism. But the transcendentalist thinkers embraced him because transcendentalism taught that one should take charge of one's own life and should not listen to institutions or organizations but act solely in accordance with one's own conscience.

And that was John Brown—a man ready to fight and kill for what he believed was right. Brown, who was raising money to fight in Kansas, made a positive impression in Concord. In February 1857, Emerson wrote in his journal, "Captain John Brown of Kansas gave a good account of himself in the Town Hall, last night, to a meeting of citizens." It was a sign of the times that Brown could give himself an unearned military rank.

Thomas Wentworth Higginson wrote, "'Old Brown' of Kansas is now in Boston . . . raising and arming a company of men for the future protection of Kansas. He wishes to raise $30,000 to arm a company, . . . but [he] will, as I understand him, take what money he can raise and use it as far as it will go."

Brown established his relationships mostly with transcendentalists. George Luther Stearns pledged his support to Brown. His wife, Mary, urged her husband to liquidate his entire fortune and give it to Brown. Stearns was chairman of the Massachusetts State Kansas Committee and on the board of the National Kansas Committee. He had raised $48,000 for Kansas, and Mary had raised another $20,000 through women's auxiliaries. Brown knew how to pitch his prospects. George was the epitome of the "self-made man," and that is what he respected. In 1907 George's son, Frank Preston Stearns, wrote a biography of his father in which he claimed that when Brown first approached George Stearns in 1857, he presented himself as a successful sheep farmer.

On the same trip, Brown met twenty-six-year-old Franklin Sanborn, a somewhat eccentric young man with refined manners, who had declared himself an abolitionist at the age of nine. He lived in Concord and was a passionate transcendentalist close to Waldo Emerson.

Sanborn, a Concord school teacher, did not have the resources of Gerrit Smith or George Stearns. But he had connections. He was the secretary of the Massachusetts State Kansas Committee, which had provided funds and arms for the Kansas struggle. Sanborn introduced Brown to Theodore Parker. He also introduced him to Samuel Howe.

Parker threw a reception for Brown, at which the rough-hewn country man was visibly uncomfortable. To Brown, everyone was too fancy and too well-dressed. This was the event at which he met Garrison and had the famous duel between Old and New Testament. Wendell Phillips also did not have a favorable impression of Brown. Thoreau, on the other hand, thought Brown had so much power and self-assurance that he didn't need his help.

Higginson was an easier sell because he was now looking for men of action like Brown. He called Brown a "genuine warrior of the Revolution."

Though Brown raised some money and two hundred Sharps rifles in Boston, he was dissatisfied with the trip. To him, these Boston abolitionists were rich people who could do more. In a farewell public letter, he wrote "Old Brown's Farewell:" "To the Plymouth Rocks, Bunker Hill Monuments, Charter Oaks, and Uncle Tom's Cabins." "Brown," he said bitterly, "has left for Kansas."

———

In 1859 Brown renewed his relations with the transcendental-ists who had supported him before. But he did not pick up any new supporters. Kansas had adopted a free-state constitution in 1859. The free-state side had won. The Union had survived. The Kansas war was over, just a skirmish after all. And yet Potawat-tomie Brown was coming to Boston asking for guns and money again. Why?

*Photo of Thomas Wentworth Higginson as Colonel of the
1st South Carolina Volunteers during the Civil War.*

Fourteen

1859—
THE WEIRD METEOR
OF WAR

Hidden in the cap
Is the anguish none can draw;
So your future veils its face,
Shenandoah!
But the streaming beard is shown
(Weird John Brown),
The meteor of the war.

—Herman Melville,
"The Portent (1859)," 1866

The year 1859 could not be called a time of optimism or "good feelings," but it was a moment with a vague sense of hope. At least there was no longer a conflict in Kansas that seemed that it was going to slide the nation into a full-scale civil war. So when bushy-bearded John Brown showed up in Boston with his new biblical look, the embodiment of that bad time that seemed over, the few in the Boston Clique who still clung to nonresistance, such as Garrison and Phillips, were filled with dread. The abolitionists, chiefly transcendentalists, who had given up on moral suasion—such as Parker, Stearns, Higginson, and Howe—were curious.

Brown was working out his idea. It showed the signs of a hastily made plan, but Brown had actually been thinking about it for decades. "This plan had occupied his thoughts and prayers for twenty years," Brown's wife later told Higginson.

In February 1858 Brown had spent three weeks in the Rochester home of Frederick Douglass. As Douglass was the most respected Black man in America, Brown reasoned that with his backing, he would have the support of the free Blacks in Boston and around the North, which had so far eluded him. In fact, he had very few supporters at all.

While staying with Douglass, Brown wrote a new Constitution. By 1859, rejection of the Constitution had wide acceptance among abolitionists. But Brown's constitution would not gain him followers because it underscored how eccentric he was. In fact, later, when Brown was on trial, his defense attorney, Samuel Chilton, used the Brown constitution to argue insanity. Brown's constitution was laudable in its insistence on complete racial equality. But then it had odd Brownisms. Profanity was illegal, as was intoxication, and an official who got drunk could be removed from office. It denounced "unlawful intercourse of the sexes." It outlawed quarreling and discouraged divorce. Religious schools were to be established. All those "known to be of good character, and of sound mind and suitable age," both men and women, were encouraged to carry firearms.

Brown trusted Douglass and he was the one person to whom he confided his plan, complete with maps and diagrams. Brown aimed to attack a federal arsenal in Virginia and use the captured weapons to arm a slave uprising he intended to incite. Douglass found Brown frightening, not just for what he was saying but the calm, matter-of-fact way in which he explained his plan to unleash violence. Once after dinner, Brown quietly explained to Douglass that "slaveholders had forfeited their right to live." His plan did not make sense to Douglass. Black people were not going to simply rise up at the arrival of this white man and his plan.

A former slave, Douglass understood that slaves were too cynical and distrusting to follow Brown's plan. A slave revolt led by a white man would not be trusted by slaves. And if carried out, Douglass termed the plan "suicide." Many Black people would be killed. He pointed at the map to explain why Brown had no chance of holding these indefensible positions. The plan could not succeed. But Brown had never been interested in success, only in his destiny. Bloodshed was the only way to end slavery, and this would unleash violent emancipation—he was certain of it.

Brown wanted not only Douglass's support but also his participation. At forty-one, Douglass was not ready to die, nor did he want to encourage others to throw away their lives. He would not support the project. Though he rejected Brown's plan, he wrote an editorial, "The Ballot and the Bullet," saying that action had to be taken, and if emancipation could not be accomplished through political means, then violence would be necessary.

Brown now had six affluent or influential supporters, known in history as "the Secret Six," though this seems to have been a misnomer, since everyone in the movement appeared to know who they were.

All but Gerrit Smith were from Boston. Whatever Smith lacked in emotional stability, he made up for in tremendous financial resources. The Boston five—Stearns, Howe, Higginson, Parker, and Sanborn—were transcendentalists.

The six did not seem to know much about Brown's plan. They believed that he planned to attack a plantation in Virginia, freeing many slaves, who he would organize into a guerrilla force, hiding in the mountains and periodically raiding plantations. Brown had been talking about this idea for years, at one time planning it in Louisiana. But as the event drew closer, Brown revealed that the current target was not to be a slave plantation but a heavily guarded federal arsenal. His supporters were not happy. But Brown argued that if he and his men died, that would do much to advance the cause. He was more interested in martyrdom than success. Douglass was right. It was suicidal.

Brown's choice of the arsenal at Harpers Ferry for a target was more symbolic than practical. There was not a large slave population there, so he was not likely to liberate large numbers. It was an attack on the federal government. This little town of five thousand, at the convergence of the Potomac River with the Shenandoah, was one of the primary manufacturing sites for US Army firearms and ammunition. The army would be obliged to call out its force, and being defeated by his liberated slaves would "strike terror into the heart of the slave States," a statement that leaves little doubt that Brown's intention was to be a terrorist in the modern sense of the word: to spread terror for the advancement of a political agenda.

Late at night on October 16, 1859, Brown and his twenty-two men, Black and white, including five family members, took the arsenal. From the beginning, nothing was the way it was supposed to be. The first man killed by Brown's forces was Hayward Shepherd, a free Black baggage handler on the Baltimore & Ohio Railroad. As the raid began, two of Brown's men crossing the bridge over the Potomac happened across Shepherd and ordered him to stop. Probably having no idea who they were or what was happening, Shepherd continued walking and they shot him. Shepherd was well-liked, and the killing infuriated both the Black and white townspeople.

Within thirty-six hours, the raid was over, and Brown and his surviving force and some thirty hostages he had taken were trapped in the Harpers Ferry engine house. In the trial, the hostages testified that they had been well treated. As Douglass had predicted, slaves did not join with them. There was no slave uprising, possibly because no slaves knew of the plan.

Three slaves who Brown claimed to have liberated were then killed in the fighting. Nine militiamen or marines were wounded, one killed. The Mayor of Harpers Ferry, unbeknownst to Brown, the rare Virginia official known for his kindness to Blacks, was also shot by Brown's men. Four other people from the town were also killed. Local militia and United States Marines under Robert E. Lee crushed Brown's small force. Ten of Brown's men were killed; others were captured, including the severely wounded Brown. Only five escaped; the rest, including Brown, were to be hanged.

As newspaper articles in Boston started identifying Brown's "secret" supporters, Sam Howe urged George Stearns to join him in fleeing to Canada. Howe, from the safety of Canada, sent a statement to the *New York Herald* asserting his shock at what Brown had done. He had thought he was a calm and reasonable man. None of this was true. He knew Brown was not calm and reasonable, and while he may not have known that Harpers Ferry was the target, he knew Brown was collecting weapons and planning something violent.

Frequently falsely reported as the man behind the conspiracy, Frederick Douglass decided it was time for him to leave when he learned authorities were coming to Rochester to interrogate him. From Canada, he left for England.

When Robert E. Lee took Brown and his surviving group, he found letters showing a tie between Brown and Frank Sanborn. Sanborn burned all letters and documents related to Brown. Marshals went to arrest him, but hundreds of Concord residents, including Waldo Emerson, came out on the street and drove the marshals off.

Smith, in the family tradition, lost his mind. He kept shouting that he was going to be indicted. Then he became gripped by guilt over the violence that he abhorred. He said he was going to Virginia to join Brown in prison. Five days after Brown was condemned to death, Smith checked himself in at the New York State Asylum for the Insane in Utica and remained there for almost two months. Then, and for the rest of his life, he denied any close connection to Brown. Later, he several times threatened lawsuits when it was written that he was one of Brown's supporters.

Higginson and Parker, the only two deeply committed to transcendentalism, held their ground and were angry at the others. They praised the raid even though it had failed. Higginson observed correctly that Brown would be more effective as a martyr than he had ever been as a military commander.

Maria Child was appalled by the raid but soon began to read accounts of Brown's comportment in captivity and started to see him as a sympathetic figure. Maria wrote to Virginia governor Henry Wise, asking permission to visit Brown. Wise was a headstrong politician who had begun his career in 1833 by severely wounding his opponent for Congress in a duel. Reaffirming her abolitionist sentiments, Maria pointed out in her letter to the governor that abolitionists did not support Brown's actions and promised not to promote abolitionism while she was in Virginia. Wise responded politely that she had a constitutional right to visit the prisoner and that the state would protect her. But Maria was not content to leave it at that. She wrote back, "Your constitutional obligation, for which you profess so much respect, has never proved any protection to citizens of the free States who happened to have a black, brown, or yellow complexion; nor to any white citizens whom you even suspected of entertaining opinions opposite to your own."

The exchange, of course, was published in newspapers. She was making her points, though they were moot, because she was not going to visit Brown.

Child wrote to Brown full of warmth and ambivalence:

Believing in peace principles, I cannot sympathize with the method you chose to advance the cause of freedom. But I honor your generous intentions,—I admire your courage, moral and physical.

She went on to volunteer her service as a nurse for his serious wounds and ended by saying,

May you be strengthened by the conviction that no honest man ever sheds blood for freedom in vain, however much he may be mistaken in his efforts.

Brown, who detested her "peace principles," politely turned her down. He told his lawyer that he did not want any women around him, including his wife, because it might undo the cool and steady façade he wanted to show. This trial and execution were to be his great performance, his one great success.

The initial reactions to the Harpers Ferry raid among Boston abolitionists were not favorable. Maria Child, who denounced his violence, asked Whittier to write a poem celebrating Harpers Ferry as the Concord that started a new revolution. It was a somewhat odd request from someone who had spent decades hoping to avoid a coming civil war. In any event, Whittier refused, saying it went against his principles. "As friends of peace, as well as friends of freedom," the Quaker poet wrote her, "as believers in the Sermon on the Mount, we dare not lend any countenance to such attempts as Harpers Ferry." He had written a poem, "Brown of Ossawatomie" (Ossawatomie is the town—Pottawatomie is the creek):

Perish with him the folly that seeks through evil good!

Garrison, in *The Liberator*, initially gave Brown a negative review, saying that his raid was "misguided, wild, and apparently insane." Then he added that it was "well intended." For once, Garrison was with the mainstream. Most northerners condemned the raid. The Republican Party, which was the antislavery party, denounced Brown. Lincoln said that the raid was an act of "violence, bloodshed, and treason." Adin Ballou unequivocally condemned Harpers Ferry and the rising tide of what he called "pro-war anti-slavery." But he admitted that true nonresistants were becoming fewer and fewer.

As soon as he was captured, the public started hearing from a new, kinder and gentler Brown. Though it contradicted the life story of Pottawatomie Brown, he seemed well-prepared for his new role. He was playing to posterity. Brown began winning support with the first interview the day after his capture, originally in the *New York Herald* and reprinted in many other papers, including *The Liberator*. In this interview, he argued that the rights of the poor and weak should be respected as much as those of the wealthy. "I pity the poor in bondage that have none to help them; that is why I am here; not to gratify any personal animosity, revenge, or vindictive spirit." He denied that he had wanted to start a general uprising of the slaves, and continued to deny it during his trial, despite the fact that he had been talking about doing that very thing for the past twenty years. He said he just wanted to set small groups free "from time to time."

Garrison, Phillips, and other nonviolent abolitionists, regardless of what they personally thought of the raid, began to realize that once Brown was hanged, he would become an invaluable martyr for the cause of abolition. Emerson said that hanging Brown would be "a terrible losing day for all Slavedom." He wrote that Brown was "the new Saint awaiting his martyrdom, and who, if he shall suffer, will make the gallows glorious like the cross." Gone was the ethos toward Lovejoy that a man who took up arms could not be a Christian martyr. But perhaps the honest sentiment was put most succinctly by Frederick Douglass, who said that he was "glad to use the event at Harpers Ferry" to awaken "the benumbed conscience of the nation."

The State of Virginia was trying to use the trial as a warning to anyone who tried to invade the South. Instead, they were turning this man, who had been seen as a lunatic, into a hero.

Brown was wise about how to play this trial—the role of a life-time—and Virginia was very foolish. Their final mistake was not neutralizing him with a pardon. Garrison somewhat callously predicted that he would do more good executed than pardoned. Even Brown, who clearly knew what he was doing, told his brother, "I am worth inconceivably more to hang than for any other purpose." But before that, Virginia made numerous other mistakes.

The first mistake was trying him before his wounds had healed. It is in the Christian tradition for the martyr to be bleeding. Brown lay bleeding on a pallet in the courtroom for the entire trial so that it appeared that the state would not allow him time to heal so he could mount a solid defense. It seemed to be a rush to judgment. The judge would not even delay one day to give time for his lawyer to arrive.

Perhaps their greatest mistake was allowing Brown to play out his new role. He wrote hundreds of letters, the eloquence of which justified Thoreau's praise of his rough but powerful writing style. These moving letters were republished throughout the northern press and created Brown fans. Furthermore, for anyone who could observe or report on the proceedings, he was soft-spoken and polite to his jailors and his prosecutors. He was a gentleman. Those who did interview him, watch the proceedings, or read about it, were struck by his grace and calm and by his quietly held but firm beliefs.

Incredibly, as though trying to give opportunities for the new John Brown to present himself, the prosecution asked, "Upon what principle do you justify your acts?" The answer was remembered for decades. "Upon the golden rule. . . . It is my sympathy for the oppressed and wronged, that are as good as you and as precious in the sight of God." Was this not a man to be admired, even emulated?

Four days before his execution, Maria Child wrote to Maria Chapman about Brown, "What a success he has made of failure, by the moral grandeur of his own character!" Even Wise was impressed with Brown. He questioned him for three hours and was surprised not to find a ranting lunatic. The governor reported, "He is cool, collected and indomitable, and he inspired me with great trust in his integrity as a man of truth." There was no doubt about Brown's guilt, and the sentence—life imprisonment, hanging, or pardon—was in the hands of the governor. Though some advised him to pardon or give a life sentence, not to make Brown a martyr who would unify the North against them, the politically ambitious Wise, whose loyalty to the South was sometimes questioned for an allegedly weak stance on Kansas and his frequent criticism of the unproductive indolence of the planter class, felt he needed to yield to the popular demand in the South to hang him.

Margaretta Mason, wife of Virginia senator James Mason who was hated in the North for authoring the Fugitive Slave Act, wrote Maria Child a vitriolic denunciation for her support of "a murderer."

Child wrote a carefully reasoned reply, explaining the argument against slavery, asserting that it was damaging the economic health of Virginia, and hurting both whites and Blacks. Mason published the correspondence in southern papers and so Child published it in the North. It was her finest writing on the slavery question since her 1833 *Appeal*, her last attempt at moral suasion, and it brought her a mountain of hate mail, most of which she characterized as "obscene."

From Canada, Howe had contemplated a plan where men would break into the jail with grenades and rescue Brown.

Higginson also hatched a plan for a rescue, but Brown rejected it saying, "I am worth inconceivably more to hang than for any other purpose."

The Boston Clique had been turned in every direction. By Thanksgiving, they could hardly think of anything but Brown's execution. They had been repelled by his random violence and moved by his comportment and dedication to abolition. And for many years, Garrison and most Garrisonians had been opposed to capital punishment. This was a killing carried out by the state of Virginia.

On December 2, Brown was taken from jail. According to legend—even illustrated by newspaper artists—he took time to greet a Black child, but this could not have been true. His arms were tied behind him and he was surrounded by military escort. John Wilkes Booth had managed to slip into a front-row seat with a contingent of Virginia Military Institute cadets. He had wanted to be there out of his intense jealousy of his brother, Edwin Booth, a far more successful actor, who had struck up a friendship with Sam Howe, now known as a Brown supporter. But he was so shaken by Brown's calm demeanor that he turned pale and trembled and was asked if he were ill.

Robert E. Lee, who had captured Brown, was there. Thomas J. "Stonewall" Jackson, later a leading Confederate general, was standing near Booth. There they all were, the faces of violence that would soon be America's tragic fate.

Daguerreotype of Wendell Phillips, 1853, by Mathew Brady.

Fifteen

1863—
RED HANDED SLAUGHTER

Red Handed Slaughter his revenge shall feed,
And Havoc yell his ominous death-cry,
And wild Despair in vain for mercy plead—
While hell itself shall shrink, and sicken at
the deed!

—from the first issue of *The Liberator*,
January 1, 1831, on the consequence
of not ending slavery peacefully

From John Brown's execution on December 2, 1859, until Lincoln issued the Emancipation Proclamation on January 1, 1863, marks the period of the most intense infighting in the thirty-year history of the Boston Clique. After his execution, Captain Brown became a hero, a patron saint of abolitionist violence. Abolitionists tried to avoid the obvious issue of Brown's violence. They did not even discuss Brown a great deal. His execution was a day to talk about the barbarism of slavery, a day to use the martyrdom more than the martyr.

On the day he was executed, throughout the North, where the raid had been denounced, church bells tolled, flags flew at half-mast, and buildings were draped in black bunting. The American Anti-Slavery Society called for meetings throughout the North to be "a moral demonstration against the bloody and merciless slave system."

In Boston, Garrison gave one of his all-time most powerful abolitionist speeches and did not even mention Brown. This was a good opportunity to talk abolitionism and not to be side-tracked by the John Brown debate. He called for disunion, separating from the South: "God forbid that we should any longer continue the accomplices of thieves and robbers, of men-stealers and women-whippers!"

Then he pleaded with the South, the last gasp of moral suasion: "What is it that God requires of the South to remove every root of bitterness, to allay every fear, to fill her borders with prosperity? But one simple act of justice, without violence and convulsion, without danger and hazard. It is this: 'Undo the heavy burdens, break every yoke, and let the oppressed go free!' Then shall thy light break forth as the morning, and thy darkness shall be as the noonday. Then shalt thou call and the Lord shall answer; thou shalt cry, and he shall say: 'Here I am.'"

At a meeting in Worcester, Abby Kelley tangled with Adin Ballou. Abby said, ambiguously, that she "agreed with John Brown in a certain sense and in another sense disagreed." Ballou attacked her for abandoning the principle of moral suasion, to which she countered by asking him what he would do if his wife were kidnapped by slavers and taken south and an armed band of Worcester men were marching off to save her. She asked him if he would say, "Don't go, but stay here. I have a lesson to teach you against shedding of blood?"

While Ballou wrote an editorial titled, "Are Non-Resistants for Murder?" Abby wrestled with an inner conflict. She recognized Brown's violence and neither approved of it nor criticized it, simply adding, "All we can say to the people is 'Oppose slavery with all your soul and strength and use such means as you can conscientiously and effectively adopt.'" Her husband, Stephen Foster, wrote in *The Liberator* in 1860, "I claim to be a Non-Resistant, but not to be a fool."

Foster rejected the idea of disunion and, to the dismay of his wife, Garrison, and others from the Clique, tried to form a separate political party for the 1860 presidential election whose platform was immediate abolition. His slogan was "Revolution, Not Dissolution." He held a convention in Boston to organize the party. Most of the Clique, including Abby, did not attend. Wendell Phillips went, but only to denounce the plan.

Garrison distrusted Lincoln but adopted what has come to be known as the lesser-of-two-evils strategy. It was going to be either Lincoln or the Democrats, and there was no doubt in Garrison's mind that Lincoln would be preferable.

While southerners were in near hysteria about Brown, with many calling for secession, the southern word for disunion, the Republican Party was trying to assuage them with firm condemnations of Brown. The 1860 Republican Party platform stated that Brown was "the gravest of criminals." Lincoln, their candidate, said that Brown's raid was "an absurd" attempt for a white man to foment a slave revolt. Few, not even Frederick

Douglass, would have argued with that. Lincoln had a genius for framing arguments in a way that was hard to refute.

Wendell Phillips, who had criticized the raid, became a Brown supporter after the hanging because he valued the symbolism. He went to New York to help Brown's widow collect the body that had been sent from Virginia. The plan was to persuade the widow to let him take the body to Boston, where it would be used to recruit abolitionists. But Phillips, after meeting her, decided this would be cruel and distasteful and abandoned the plan.

After Brown's execution, Thoreau, who even today is remembered for his stands against war and violence, wrote "A Plea for Captain John Brown." He wrote that Brown was an exception to his belief in nonviolence: "I do not wish to kill nor to be killed, but I can foresee circumstances in which both these things would be by me unavoidable. . . . I think that for once the Sharp's rifles and the revolvers were employed in a righteous cause." Thoreau went so far as to write that Brown had "a spark of divinity in him"—a surprising assertion from a man who did not accept the divinity of Jesus Christ.

Waldo Emerson wrote of Thoreau in the sardonic style for which he had become famous, "This exciting theme seemed to have awakened 'the hermit of Concord' from his usual state of philosophic indifference."

Thoreau criticized Garrison for questioning Brown's sanity in *The Liberator*: "What though he did not belong to your clique! Though you may not approve of his method or his principles, recognize his magnanimity."

And it is true that Garrison should have known better than most to be careful with such labels since they were often used against him. In 1837 he had written to a New Hampshire newspaper editor, "Remember that LIBERTY is crucified in your country, and all her true worshippers are branded as madmen, fanatics, and incendiaries!"

Brown, the onetime pariah of abolitionism, was becoming its leading symbol. Even the great voice of the French conscience, Victor Hugo, praised John Brown.

Emerson still had his reservations. "John Brown has, perhaps, a right to a place by the side of Moses, Joshua, Gideon and David; but he is not on the same plane with Jesus, Paul, Peter and John, the weapons of whose warfare were not carnal," he wrote. Again, Old versus New Testament. Many Quakers remained critical, including Lucretia Mott, even though she took Brown's wife into her home for comfort during the trial. Whittier also remained critical.

The legend of John Brown grew after his death. So did he. Contemporaries usually described him as being of average height, certainly not as tall as Douglass, Phillips, Howe, or Higginson. But after his death, he was almost always described as "tall."

Higginson, recognizing that Brown's way was the way of the future, began studying military books and "took notes on fortifications, strategy, and the principles of attack and defense."

In the 1860 presidential election, Abraham Lincoln won eighteen of thirty-three states. He was deeply unpopular in the South, so much so that in order to assume office, he was slipped into Washington from Maryland in a disguise to foil any possible assassination attempt. While Lincoln, in the view of northern abolitionists, was far from an abolitionist, that was how the South saw him. Lincoln was the only antislavery president except for the Massachusetts father and son Adams, both of whom were unpopular one-term presidents.

Southerners were used to getting their way, controlling the White House and often the Congress. Now that was finished. In addition to the White House, Lincoln's Republican Party controlled 106 of the 183 seats in the House and held a narrow majority in the Senate.

While the South was certain Lincoln intended to end slavery, northern abolitionists were not at all sure. For the Boston Clique, Lincoln was as divisive a figure as John Brown. After Lincoln's election, Wendell Phillips went on a speaking campaign to assert that the election meant the end of slavery, which was more of a hope than a reality. He was trying to pressure Lincoln. And it was exactly what Lincoln did not want to tell the South. Later, some in the South Carolina legislature claimed that it was Phillips's speeches that convinced them that secession was necessary.

Many in the Boston Clique thought this was the time to act. Maria Child wrote Francis Shaw from Medford in January 1861, "My own belief is, that if the North would only show a bold, united front now, despotism would quail before it, and be compelled to become subordinate to freedom; and if once subordinated, it must ere long cease to be."

But there was not a united front. Not everyone in Boston was pleased by Phillips's speeches. Trade with the South was slacking off, leading to a number of mill and factory closings, and industrialists and workers were angry. Industrialists pleaded with Washington to be moderate and avoid a civil war. In Boston, they encouraged workers to riot, and the police clearly sided with the mob. The mobocracy of the 1830s had come back to Boston, shouting down Phillips, threatening violence. Maria Child and Maria Chapman escorted Phillips, one on each side, to an event, because the mob would hesitate to attack women. That did not always work. On one occasion, Maria Child was physically molested by a rioter when leaving a Phillips speech at the Boston Music Hall. She turned to one of her well-dressed assailants and began lecturing him on his behavior until he agreed to act better.

Southerners did not want to live in a country dominated by northerners. Even before the final election results, southerners were calling for secession. This made some sense to Boston abolitionists who had been calling for disunion for the past twenty years. On the day of Brown's execution, Garrison said, "Would to heaven they would go! It would only be the paupers clearing out from the town, would it not?" In the January 4 *Liberator*, he hailed it and predicted the collapse of the slave system without northern support. Most of the abolitionists were happy to see the South go. For years, that had been their cry. What would have happened if the Union just let them go? According to Garrison, the slaves would have risen up, as in Haiti, and the South by itself would not have been strong enough to put down the revolt. But some abolitionists argued that it would be wrong for the North to abandon the enslaved people of the South.

Garrison, and many abolitionists, saw civil war as a huge mistake. He had no doubt the North could defeat the South militarily and force them to free their slaves. But the North could not "conquer her spirit or change her determination." If they could not change their thinking, how was this ever going to end?

The southern idea of secession was very different from the abolitionist idea of peaceful disunion, a negotiated separation. To the South, the tool for secession was military force. South Carolina attacked an army base in Charleston Harbor, Fort Sumter, and the war the Boston Clique had always tried to avoid, began. Ironically, that same month, Governor Wise, who had hanged Brown for treason, pushed Virginia toward secession by raising a force that attacked the arsenal in Harpers Ferry.

Many abolitionists opposed the war. Vermont abolitionist Beriah Green wrote in *The Liberator*, May 17, 1861, a month after the war had begun, "Freedom, in any proper sense of the inspiring word, is not the child of violence."

Wendell Phillips distrusted Lincoln and did not support the war. And his wife Ann complained to him that he did not stand up enough against the supporters of the war. Abby Kelley and Stephen Foster denounced the war, saying, "If you are battling with slavery upon the field of blood, you are not on my platform." Adin Ballou actively opposed the war and denounced his old friend and colleague, Garrison, for not resisting it. He called it "absurd twaddle" that Christians should kill their enemies. Surprisingly, it was Garrison who urged abolitionist opposition to be tempered by restraint.

Frederick Douglass called the war "The Slaveholders' Rebellion" and termed the fact that some abolitionists were still dreaming of peace "this infatuation, this blindness to the significance of passing events." He believed the Civil War would end slavery and he called this doing it "the John Brown way."

Maria Child could not support a war dedicated to reestablishing the Union she had wanted to see broken. Some Garrisonians held firmly to the belief that war would not give Black people their rights. Abby Kelley wrote in *The Liberator*, "the hate of the colored race will still continue, and the poison of that wickedness will destroy us as a nation."

The central problem for abolitionists was Lincoln. As late as the 1850s he was still talking of colonization. In his second famous debate with Stephen A. Douglas in 1858, he had said that he did not favor equality of the races and did not want Blacks to get the vote. In a letter to Horace Greeley, on August 12, 1862, he wrote: "If I could save the union without freeing any slaves I would do it; and if I could save it by freeing all the slaves, I would do it; and if I could save it by freeing some and leaving others alone, I would also do that."

This was the opposite of the Boston Clique's point of view. They did not care about saving the Union and didn't think it was worth saving unless slavery was abolished. Garrison called Lincoln "a slow coach" but thought he would come around in time. Maria Child agreed with him. But Phillips did not, and there was beginning to be a serious rift between Phillips and Garrison, also Ballou and Garrison.

And what was Senator Charles Sumner doing—the nonresistant abolitionist, still Vice President of the American Peace Society, the man who in 1845 had argued that all constitutions were flawed because they allowed war, "which is a sin as hateful and mischievous as that of slavery"? He was Lincoln's close ally in the Senate, working in pursuit of the war.

Here was the living example of the claim made by so many in the Boston Clique that once you enter government you can no longer be nonresistant. Sumner believed that he could pursue the war and still be a pacifist on the tenuous position that violence was unacceptable, except in matters of self-defense. Many nonresistants accepted self-defense, but it is a difficult road. Doesn't the slave have the right to defend himself against the violence of the slaveholder? Isn't a war permissible if a country is attacked?

Sumner remained opposed to war, but as a senator, he had to allow an exception: a country, like an individual, had the right to defend itself, for example, when attacked. Garrison said this argument for defensive war was a trap, since everyone claims their war is defensive. His point was illustrated when the Civil War broke out and both the North and the South claimed defensive war. The North argued that the South had fired on northern troops, and the South argued that they were being invaded by northern troops.

Clausewitz in *On War* does not concern himself with defensive war. He wrote that a supposedly defensive war does not remain defensive for long. He defined war as "an act of violence intended to compel our opponent to fulfill our will." This was Garrison's point—the South might be compelled to end slavery, but that did not mean they would agree with it. Clausewitz also wrote, "The result in war is never absolute." And this was what was worrying abolitionists.

One of the best illustrations of Abraham Lincoln's political genius is the 1863 Emancipation Proclamation, in which he declared his commitment to ending slavery and, in the same stroke, avoided freeing any slaves. Until then, to the fury of abolitionists, the war had only been about preserving the Union. Now he wanted the moral weight of a commitment to ending slavery—eventually. He did not want to alienate the four states—Maryland, Delaware, Kentucky, and Missouri—that allowed slavery but had sided with the Union. So he proclaimed that he was freeing slaves in territories controlled by the Confederacy. Since he could not accomplish this, in the short term, the proclamation did not free any slaves.

The Emancipation Proclamation might not have freed slaves, but it certainly splintered and destabilized the abolitionist movement. In 1862, when Lincoln had first floated the idea of an emancipation proclamation, Garrison had found it too moderate. But in January 1863, the day after it was released, Garrison wrote in *The Liberator*, "It is a great historic event, sublime in its magnitude." To Phillips it was a sham and did nothing to end slavery. Within a few months, Garrison had grown impatient and, like Phillips, was calling for stronger measures. But the tension between Garrison and Phillips was growing. At the heart of the disagreement, Garrison trusted Lincoln and admired him and Phillips didn't. This came out at every meeting where the two were present. Phillips would denounce Lincoln and then Garrison would defend him. Phillips argued that the *Standard* was too pro-Lincoln, and Garrison argued that it was being fair and balanced.

Finally, in 1864, Garrison met the president, and he liked him. Lincoln complimented Garrison on his youthful appearance and joked about the fact that the prison in Baltimore that held Garrison in 1830 had been torn down. "Then you could not get out of prison, now you cannot get in," quipped the president. Garrison was charmed by the way Lincoln laughed at his own jokes. Garrison did that too. But the following day, in deeper discussions, Garrison was impressed with a deep, underlying intelligence in this man posing as a country bumpkin.

Garrison, the radical leader, was becoming more moderate and Phillips was becoming more radical. In 1862 Phillips said in a speech, "the President holds out his hands to the people and says, 'Am I right?' 'How far may I go?' Answer him. Tell him 'the ice is thick thus far.'" A year after the Emancipation Proclamation, Garrison seemed even more moderate. He wrote, "the President has been steadily advancing toward the goal of liberty, and perhaps quite as fast as the altered state of the Northern mind will allow him."

The Emancipation Proclamation did have a number of significant accomplishments. It declared at last that the war was about ending slavery. In doing this, Lincoln had neutralized England and France, who were considering siding with the Confederacy to gain a new foothold in North America. Now, to do that would appear to be supporting slavery, which was politically unacceptable to their populations. The Proclamation also meant that as the Union Army took territory, they would emancipate slaves. Up until then, Union troops often turned liberated Black people back over to slave owners. Lincoln now called for the organization of "colored regiments" with white officers to serve in combat.

General Ulysses S. Grant was in favor of Black regiments even before the Proclamation, and many abolitionists backed this idea even though it quashed the stand of nonresistance. The first Black regiment, the 1st South Carolina Volunteer Infantry Regiment, was mustered in 1862. It was commanded by Colonel Thomas Higginson, who was eager to test the theories of warfare he had been studying. But the regiment did not participate in any major battles. Comprised of escaped slaves from Florida and South Carolina, they were effective raiders along the Georgia and Florida coastlines.

The 1st Kansas Colored Infantry Regiment was also created in 1862 with Black officers, but in 1863, after the Proclamation, when the unit was mustered into the Union Army, none of the three Black officers were given commissions. The 1st Kansas did see battles and suffered enormous losses.

In 1863 the first regiment of predominantly free Black men was created, the 54th Massachusetts Volunteer Infantry Regiment. The 54th was assembled in Boston and free Blacks from all over New England and beyond came to enlist. Volunteering to serve was seen as an important step toward equal rights and a source of pride that outweighed ideas of pacifism. In fact, it was a huge blow to nonresistance, especially among free Blacks. Leading Blacks, former pacifists, including Frederick Douglass, William Nell, and Charles Lenox Remond recruited volunteers for the 54th. Two of Douglass's sons, Charles Remond Douglass and Lewis Henry Douglass, traveled to Boston and volunteered.

Massachusetts governor John Andrew commissioned the son of Maria Child's close friends, Sarah and Francis Shaw, Robert Gould Shaw, to serve as colonel of the 54th. Robert Shaw had not been a nonresistant and in 1863, he already had some combat experience and had been wounded at Antietam as a lieutenant in the 2nd Massachusetts Infantry Regiment. Twice wounded, he was promoted to captain. He was hesitant to accept this new commission as colonel of the 54th because he did not believe Black regiments would be allowed an important combat role. His parents persuaded him, and he rigorously trained the 54th for combat.

Boston turned out one of its largest crowds in history to cheer the 54th as they marched off to war down State Street to ship out at the waterfront. The band was playing "John Brown's Body," which was becoming a marching song of the Union Army. The song was created in Boston in 1861 by a quartet accompanying the drilling of the Boston Light Infantry in Boston Harbor. According to W. E. B. Du Bois, the tune came from "an old camp meeting tune—possibly of Negro origin," called "Say, Brother, Will You Meet Us?" The message of the song is that while Brown is dead, his soul lives on in the Union Army.

Standing on the corner of Wilson's Lane and State Street to see the 54th off to war with the soul of John Brown, Garrison realized he was in the very spot where he had been dragged by a rope in 1835. He did not share the enthusiasm of most of the Boston crowd. There was an army, raised by his fellow pacifists, marching off to kill. There were Charles and Lewis Douglass, sons of Frederick with whom he had built a nonviolent movement. And there was young Robert Shaw, son of Sarah and Francis, the boy who had played with his sons, leading this column of righteous killers. A whole young generation of pacifists was marching off to war. Nor could Maria Child cheer to see her close friend's son, a boy for whom she had babysat, leading the sons of Boston people she had known and worked with on nonresistance, off to kill. This was not turning out the way it was supposed to.

There were too many volunteers for one regiment, and the overflow from the 54th became the 55th Massachusetts Infantry Regiment. They received a smaller sendoff, but it was even more painful for Lloyd Garrison, because his son, George, volunteered as a lieutenant in the 55th. This was a blow to Lloyd, who had raised his sons to be nonresistants. His other two sons firmly opposed warfare.

Still, Garrison wrote a loving letter to George:

True, I could have wished you could ascend to what I believe a higher plane of moral heroism and a nobler method of self-sacrifice; but as you are true to yourself, I am glad of your fidelity, and proud of your willingness to run any risk in a cause that is undeniably just and good.

The 54th undertook a suicidal bayonet charge on a fort in Charleston Harbor and Shaw was killed and 250 of his 600 men were killed or wounded. Douglass's son Lewis was among the wounded. As often happens with suicidal attacks, it became famous. It settled the issue of whether Blacks would make good soldiers.

The 55th did not see major battles, and at the end of the war, they marched victoriously with Lieutenant Garrison through Charleston, singing "John Brown's Body."

Aside from slavery itself, the war was one of the greatest tragedies in American history. In a small nation with only a sixth the population of that in mid-twentieth-century America, 620,000 combatants died, more than the total American casualties of both world wars, Korea, and Vietnam combined.

Abolitionists cheered the Thirteenth Amendment when it passed Congress in 1865, outlawing slavery in the United States. But after the war was over, Stephen Foster predicted that justice for African Americans would not endure, because it had been a "forcible emancipation." It was not until 1868 that former slaves were guaranteed citizenship with the Fourteenth Amendment.

It was not until 1870 that African American men were guaranteed voting rights. Many abolitionists, including Abby Kelley, had worked hard for the amendment, but some, including Susan B. Anthony and Elizabeth Cady Stanton, opposed it because it failed to give voting rights to women, white or Black.

Before the war, Lloyd Garrison had predicted that war could not bring about real freedom and justice. At the end of the war, he celebrated that it had done so, but not without reservations. In 1865, three months after the war had ended, Garrison wrote Maria Child,

> *Slavery being abolished, and the rebellion at last suddenly suppressed, we are now in an anomalous and very complex condition, and the work of reconstruction is beset with many difficulties and dangers. But I believe we shall come out right in the end. Of course, much of the old slaveholding spirit remains, and it will try to be as insolent and cruel as possible, especially toward its former victims. It would be miraculous if it were otherwise. But this cannot last long.*

But by the 1870s, he began to see that it would last, that he had been right in the first place, that southern Blacks were being abandoned, and that "the battle of liberty and equal rights is to be fought over again."

The Boston Clique had predicted that if emancipation came about through violence, it would take at least a century for Black people to secure their rights. It has been taking even longer than that.

Charles Lenox Remond.

ILLUSIVE HISTORY

*Fame is water
carried in a basket.*
—Lalla, fourteenth-century
Kashmiri poetess

Nothing can be learned from that which is not remembered. History is unkind to those who fail, and the Boston nonviolent abolitionist movement failed spectacularly, failing to achieve moral suasion and ending in the greatest blood bath in American history. But though they failed in the short term, their influence had a long reach. History has little memory of abolitionists and even less of pacifists. The conventional view is that the slaves were freed by Abraham Lincoln and the violence of the Civil War. It is seldom noted that the strategies of the twentieth-century Civil Rights movement—nonviolence, marches, boycotts, freedom songs, restaurant sit-ins, freedom rides—were established a century earlier by the Boston Clique.

There is not one clear line by which the tactics of the Boston Clique became the tactics of Martin Luther King Jr. and the

Southern Christian Leadership Conference (SCLC), the Student Nonviolent Coordinating Committee (SNCC), or before them, groups such as James Farmer's Congress of Racial Equality (CORE). The ideas of resistance from nineteenth-century Boston traveled to the Civil Rights movement of the 1950s and 1960s through many routes. The modern Civil Rights movement was like a great delta fed by many rivers.

Novelist Leo Tolstoy, who became a great advocate for Christian nonviolence, admired the writing of Adin Ballou and William Lloyd Garrison. And he passed these writings on to Gandhi. Gandhians came to the US to teach civil rights leaders.

The women's suffrage movement came from Boston abolitionists, including Susan B. Anthony, Elizabeth Cady Stanton, and Frederick Douglass. The growing American labor movement of the late nineteenth century and early twentieth century also used many of the ideas of Boston nonresistance. Labor demonstrations (and their songs) would have felt familiar to Garrison, Phillips, Nell, Child, Douglass, and the others.

The Garrisonian nonresistance movement lived on after the Civil War—even after Garrison, who died in 1879. Directly after the Civil War, the Universal Peace Union was formed and met first in Boston and then in Providence. Adin Ballou, Lucretia Mott, Henry Wright, and even Stephen Foster, who repented having briefly supported the Civil War at its end, joined the Peace Union. They gradually replaced the American Peace Society, which, like Sumner, made an exception for defensive war. The Peace Union kept the Garrisonian principles of not participating in politics but, like the Boston Clique, argued about the idea of not voting.

The Union turned its efforts toward supporting persecuted minorities such as Blacks and Native Americans. They also supported the labor movement. In 1898 they vigorously opposed the Spanish-American War as the Garrisonians had the Mexican War. Opposing war is always unpopular, and the Union soon faded away, only to reappear in 1915 as the Fellowship of Reconciliation (FOR), which opposed World War I. The FOR leader, A. J. Muste, later helped organize Bayard Rustin, James Farmer, and George Hauser in 1942 into the Congress of Racial Equality (CORE), a nonviolent group that used such Boston tactics as sit-ins to integrate Denver movie theaters and an all-white cafeteria in Detroit. It was the beginning of the Civil Rights movement. Farmer, Rustin, and Hauser all went to prison for refusing the World War II draft. Rustin, as a Quaker, could have been exempted but chose to go to prison as a protest. In prison, they organized a sit-in to desegregate prison dining.

Though African American history has never been widely taught, it has always been taught in some places. One example is West Chester, Pennsylvania, a Quaker town that once was an important station for the Underground Railroad. In the 1920s West Chester schools were segregated. Gay Street was a Black school with a history teacher, Helena Robinson, who had graduated from Howard University. Robinson not only taught her young pupils about the Underground Railroad, arranging visits to sites that still existed in town, but she also taught them about the abolitionists eighty years earlier. One of her students was Bayard Rustin, the man who convinced Martin Luther King Jr. to turn to nonviolence.

The most remembered abolitionist, and this tells much about our society, was the most violent, John Brown. Those who know their history or know their pacifism remember William Lloyd Garrison, mostly for *The Liberator*. Frederick Douglass is remembered as a giant of African American history who stood up against slavery and was a leader on women's rights as well as the rights of Black people and Native Americans. He is also remembered for having written the best slave narratives. Paul, Nell, Remond, and other Black abolitionists did not enjoy Douglass's enduring fame.

Most of the abolitionists who are remembered are recalled for things other than abolition. Elizabeth Cady Stanton, Susan B. Anthony, and Margaret Fuller are remembered for their work on women's rights, and it is barely remembered that they were abolitionists.

Essays on transcendentalism by Henry David Thoreau and Ralph Waldo Emerson are still read, and Thoreau is remembered for his nature writing. But Thoreau also had a profound impact on nonviolent political activism. When in prison, Gandhi read Thoreau's *Civil Disobedience*, and King did the same. Mario Savio, a Berkeley student, delivered a speech in 1964 from the hood of a car that is credited with launching the student movement of the 1960s. The most remembered lines of Savio's speech about throwing your body on the machine are a paraphrase of *Civil Disobedience*.

John Greenleaf Whittier's poems are still read, especially "Snowbound," about a harsh winter storm in rural New England. It was written on his farm in Haverhill, where Garrison used to come to discuss abolitionist strategy. It is seldom recalled that Whittier was a leading abolitionist and an uncompromising advocate of nonviolence.

The only one of John Brown's Secret Six to be remembered is Samuel Gridley Howe, not for his abolitionism but for his work educating the blind. His wife, Julia Ward Howe, is remembered for her bloodthirsty "Battle Hymn of the Republic" that declares, "Let us die to make men free." Elizabeth Peabody, America's first woman publisher, is largely remembered for her work promoting kindergarten education. Horace Mann is also remembered for his work in education and not for his considerable contribution to nonresistant abolitionism. Bronson Alcott, if remembered at all, is known as the father of author Louisa May Alcott.

The great voices of nonviolence, Adin Ballou, William Ladd, and Noah Worcester, are seldom recalled, though their work lives on in the many activists they influenced.

Most of the Boston Clique are now forgotten. Lydia Maria Child was one of the most famous writers of nineteenth-century America, but her work did not survive into posterity. She is seldom read today. Her cookbook, *The American Frugal Housewife*, is studied by food historians. In all her writing, her most famous lines are from her Thanksgiving poem: "Over the river and through the wood / To grandfather's house we go." She always liked Thanksgiving.

The great leaders of nonviolence, charismatic figures such as Mohandas Gandhi and Martin Luther King Jr., are often remembered as rarefied geniuses who hatched their ideas from the ether, but the ideas and tools of nonviolent activism have been pursued by many people many times, and though a small group in nineteenth-century Boston may be little remembered today, what they did, what they learned, and what they taught, have lived on.

ACKNOWLEDGMENTS

A big thank-you to Charlotte Sheedy for bringing me to Godine, a remarkable house where I have always wanted to do a book. I am deeply grateful to Celia Johnson, whose painstaking and thoughtful work has helped me shape this book. To the memory of my uncle, Jack Solomon, who first taught me what war really was. And to Ralph DiGia, Dave Dellinger, and George Hauser—the few of the great that I had the privilege to meet and all the ones I met and those I only followed—the brave and wise I have learned from and marched with in the naïve but enduring belief that we can build a better world.

BIBLIOGRAPHY

Ballou, Adin. *Christian Non-Resistance, in All Its Important Bearings, Illustrated and Defended*. London: Charles Gilpin, 1848.

Bartlett, Irving H. *Wendell and Ann Phillips: The Community of Reform, 1840–1880*. New York: W. W. Norton, 1979.

Blight, David W. *Frederick Douglass: Prophet of Freedom*. New York: Simon & Schuster, 2018.

Brock, Peter. *Pacifism in the United States: From the Colonial Era to the First World War*. Princeton: Princeton University Press, 1968.

Cain, William E., ed. *William Lloyd Garrison and the Fight against Slavery: Selections from* The Liberator. Boston: Bedford Books of St. Martin's Press, 1995.

Chapman, Maria Weston. *Right and Wrong in Massachusetts*. Boston: Dow & Jackson's Anti-Slavery Press, 1839.

Cheever, Susan. *American Bloomsbury: Louisa May Alcott, Ralph Waldo Emerson, Margaret Fuller, Nathaniel Hawthorne, and Henry David Thoreau: Their Lives, Their Loves, Their Work*. New York: Simon & Schuster, 2006.

Chernow, Ron. *Grant*. New York: Penguin Press, 2017.

Child, David Lee. *The Culture of the Beet and Manufacture of Beet Sugar*. Boston: Weeks, Jordan, 1840.

———. *The Texan Revolution*. Washington, DC: J. and G. S. Gideon, 1843.

Child, Lydia Maria. *The American Frugal Housewife*. 12th ed. Boston: Carter, Hendee, 1833.

———. *An Appeal in Favor of That Class of Americans Called Africans*. Amherst: University of Massachusetts Press, 1996.

———. *Authentic Anecdotes of American Slavery*. 2nd ed. Newburyport: Charles Whipple, 1838.

———. *Autumnal Leaves*. New York: C. S. Francis, 1857.

———. *The Duty of Disobedience to the Fugitive Slave Act*. Boston: American Anti-Slavery Society, 1860.

———. *Fact and Fiction: A Collection of Stories*. New York: C. S. Francis, 1847.

————. *The Family Nurse.* Boston: Charles J. Hendee, 1837.

————. *The First Settlers of New-England: Or, Conquest of the Pequods, Narragansets and Pokanokets: As Related by a Mother to Her Children.* Boston: Munroe and Francis, 1829.

————. *The Girl's Own Book.* Chester, CT: Applewood Books, 1992.

————. *Hobomok and Other Writings on Indians.* Edited by Carolyn L. Karcher. New Brunswick, NJ: Rutgers University Press, 1986.

————. *Letters from New York.* Athens: University of Georgia Press, 1998.

————. *Letters of Lydia Maria Child, with a Biographical Introduction by John G. Whittier and an Appendix by Wendell Phillips.* Boston: Houghton, Mifflin; Cambridge: Riverside Press, 1883.

————. *The Mother's Book.* Boston: Carter, Hendee and Babcock, 1831.

————. *Over the River and through the Wood: A Thanksgiving Poem by Lydia Maria Child.* Illustrated by Christopher Manson. New York: North-South Books, 1993.

————. *The Rebels; Or, Boston before the Revolution.* Boston: Phillips, Sampson, 1850.

————. *The Right Way the Safe Way, Proved by Emancipation in the British West Indies and Elsewhere.* New York: n.p., 1860.

————. *A Romance of the Republic.* Boston: Ticknor and Fields, 1867.

Clifford, Deborah Pickman. *Crusader for Freedom: A Life of Lydia Maria Child.* Boston: Beacon Press, 1992.

Cromwell, Otelia. *Lucretia Mott.* Cambridge: Harvard University Press, 1958.

Daley, James, ed. *Great Speeches by Frederick Douglass.* Mineola, NY: Dover Publications, 2013.

Davis, David Brion. *The Problem of Slavery in the Age of Revolution, 1770–1823.* Ithaca: Cornell University Press, 1975.

D'Emilio, John. *Lost Prophet: The Life and Times of Bayard Rustin.* New York: Free Press, 2003.

Donald, David Herbert. *Charles Sumner and the Coming of the Civil War.* Chicago: University of Chicago Press, 1960.

Douglass, Frederick. *Life and Times of Frederick Douglass.* Radford, VA: Wilder Publications, 2008.

————. *My Bondage and My Freedom.* Mineola, NY: Dover Publications, 1969.

————. *Narrative of the Life of Frederick Douglass.* New York: Signet Classics, 1968.

Du Bois, W. E. B. *John Brown.* Oak Park, MI: New World Paper Backs, 2014.

Emerson, Ralph Waldo and Henry David Thoreau. *Transcendentalism: Essential Essays of Emerson and Thoreau.* Clayton, DE: Prestwick House, 2008.

Finkelman, Paul, ed. *His Soul Goes Marching On: Responses to John Brown and the Harpers Ferry Raid*. Charlottesville and London: University of Press of Virginia, 1995.

Fuller, Margaret. *Women in the Nineteenth Century*. Mineola, NY: Dover Publications, 1999.

Garrison, William Lloyd. *The Letters of William Lloyd Garrison*. Vol. 1. Edited by Walter M. Merrill. Cambridge: Belknap Press, 1971.

———. *The Letters of William Lloyd Garrison*. Vol. 2. Edited by Louis Ruchamps. Cambridge: Belknap Press, 1971.

———. *The Letters of William Lloyd Garrison*. Vol. 3. Edited by Walter M. Merrill. Cambridge: Belknap Press, 1973.

———. *The Letters of William Lloyd Garrison*. Vol. 4. Edited by Louis Ruchamps. Cambridge: Belknap Press, 1975.

———. *The Letters of William Lloyd Garrison*. Vol. 5. Edited by Walter M. Merrill. Cambridge: Belknap Press, 1979.

———. *The Letters of William Lloyd Garrison*. Vol. 6. Edited by Walter M. Merrill and Louis Ruchamps. Cambridge: Belknap Press, 1981.

———. *Thoughts on African Colonization*. Alberta: Okotoks Press, 2017.

———. *Words of Garrison: A Centennial Selection (1805–1905) of Characteristic Sentiments from the Writings of William Lloyd Garrison*. Boston and New York: Houghton, Mifflin; Cambridge: Riverside Press, 1905.

Gates, Henry Louis, Jr. *The Classic Slave Narratives*. New York: New American Library, 1987.

Hawthorne, Nathaniel. *The Blithedale Romance*. Boston: Ticknor and Fields, 1852.

———. *Miscellanies: Biographical and Other Sketches and Letters. Vol. 17 of The Complete Writings of Nathaniel Hawthorne*. Boston and New York: Houghton, Mifflin; Cambridge: Riverside Press, 1900.

Higginson, Thomas Wentworth. *Army Life in a Black Regiment and Other Writings*. New York: Penguin Books, 1997.

———. *Contemporaries*. Boston and New York: Houghton, Mifflin; Cambridge: Riverside Press, 1899.

Hoock, Holger. *Scars of Independence: America's Violent Birth*. New York: Broadway Books, 2017.

James, Henry. "Nathaniel Hawthorne (1804–1864)." In *Library of the World's Best Literature Ancient and Modern*, edited by Charles Dudley Warner, 7053–7061. Vol. 12. New York: R. S. Peale and J. A. Hill, 1896.

Karcher, Carolyn L. *The First Lady of the Republic: A Cultural Biography of Lydia Maria Child*. Durham: Duke University Press, 1994.

Kazin, Alfred, ed. *Selected Short Stories of Nathaniel Hawthorne.* New York: Random House, 1966.

Kenschaft, Lori. *Lydia Maria Child: The Quest For Racial Justice.* New York: Oxford University Press, 2003.

Kraditor, Aileen S. *Means and Ends in American Abolitionism: Garrison and His Critics on Strategy and Tactics, 1834–1850.* New York: Vintage Books, 1969.

Kurlansky, Mark. *Non-Violence: The History of a Dangerous Idea.* New York: Modern Library, 2006.

Mabee, Carleton. *Black Freedom: The Nonviolent Abolitionists from 1830 through the Civil War.* London: Macmillan, 1970.

Marshall, Megan. *The Peabody Sisters.* Boston: Houghton Mifflin, 2005.

Matteson, John. *The Lives of Margaret Fuller.* New York: W. W. Norton, 2012.

Mayer, Henry. *All On Fire: William Lloyd Garrison and the Abolition of Slavery.* New York: St. Martin's Press, 1998.

Meltzer, Milton and Patricia G. Holland, eds. *Lydia Maria Child: Selected Letters, 1817–1880.* Amherst: University of Massachusetts Press, 1982.

Miller, Edwin Haviland. *Salem Is My Dwelling Place: A Life of Nathaniel Hawthorne.* Iowa City: University of Iowa Press, 1991.

Miller, William Lee. *Arguing About Slavery: John Quincy Adams and the Great Battle in the United States Congress.* New York: Alfred A. Knopf, 1996.

Pacificus, Philo [Noah Worcester]. *A Solemn Review of the Custom of War.* Boston: S. G. Simpkins, 1833.

Perry, Bliss, ed. *The Heart of Emerson's Journals.* Boston and New York: Houghton Mifflin; Cambridge: Riverside Press, 1926.

Redpath, James. *Echoes of Harper's Ferry.* Boston: Thayer and Eldridge, 1860.

Renehan, Edward J., Jr. *The Secret Six: How a Circle of Northern Aristocrats Helped Light the Fuse of the Civil War.* New York: Crown Publishers, 1995.

Reynolds, David S. *John Brown: Abolitionist.* New York: Alfred A. Knopf, 2005.

Sinha, Manisha. *The Slave's Cause: A History of Abolition.* New Haven and London: Yale University Press, 2016.

Sterling, Dorothy. *Ahead of Her Time: Abby Kelley and the Politics of Antislavery.* New York: W. W. Norton, 1994.

Stewart, James Brewer, ed. *William Lloyd Garrison at Two Hundred: History, Legacy, and Memory.* New Haven and London: Yale University Press, 2008.

Stuckey, Sterling. *Slave Culture: Nationalist Theory and the Foundations of Black America.* New York and Oxford, UK: Oxford University Press, 1987.

Thomas, John L. *The Liberator, William Lloyd Garrison: A Biography.* Boston and Toronto: Little, Brown, 1963.

Thoreau, Henry David. *Civil Disobedience and Other Essays.* New York: Dover Publications, 1993.

Titone, Nora. *My Thoughts Be Bloody: The Bitter Rivalry between Edwin and John Wilkes Booth That Led to an American Tragedy.* New York: Free Press, 2010.

Walker, David. *Walker's Appeal, in Four Articles.* Delhi: Alpha Editions, 2020.

White, Maria. Letter to Sophia Peabody Hawthorne. January 1, 1845.

Wood, Gordon S. *The American Revolution.* New York: Modern Library, 2002.

IMAGE SOURCES

Prologue: Library of Congress
Chapter One: Library of Congress
Chapter Two: Alamy
Chapter Three: Alamy
Chapter Four Boston Public Library
Chapter Five: Massachusetts Historical Society
Chapter Six: Library of Congress
Chapter Seven: Alamy
Chapter Eight: Alamy
Chapter Nine: National Portrait Gallery
Chapter Ten: Library of Congress
Chapter Eleven: National Portrait Gallery
Chapter Twelve: Library of Congress
Chapter Thirteen: Library of Congress
Chapter Fourteen: Massachusetts Historical Society
Chapter Fifteen: Library of Congress
Epilogue: Massachusetts Historical Society